Unfinished Business

Unfinished Business

**The Theory and Practice
of Personal Process Work
in Training**

Neil Clark and Keri Phillips
with Dave Barker

Gower

Published by
Gower Publishing Company Limited,
Gower House,
Croft Road,
Aldershot,
Hants GU11 3HR,
England

Gower Publishing Company,
Old Post Road,
Brookfield,
Vermont 05036,
U.S.A.

British Library Cataloguing in Publication Data
Clark, Neil
  Unfinished business
  1. Personnel management   2. Interpersonal relations
  I. Title   II. Phillips, Keri
  III. Barker, Dave
  658.3'145   HF5549

  ISBN 0-566-02514-0

Library of Congress Cataloging in Publication Data
Clark, Neil
  Unfinished business
  Bibliography: p.
  Includes index.
  1. Group relations training.   2. Employees, Training of.
  3. Interpersonal relations — Study and teaching.
  I. Phillips, Keri.   II. Barker, Dave.   III. Title.
  HF5549.5.G73C57 1984   658.3'001'9   84-8134

  ISBN 0-566-02514-0

Typeset by Saxon Printing Limited, Derby
Printed and bound by Billing & Sons Limited, Worcester.

CONTENTS

PREFACE

Our principal aim in writing this book has been to describe and analyse personal process work. This is an approach to training which has become increasingly important for us, both personally and professionally in recent years. It is also clear to us that trainers have shown growing interest in personal process work and it is our hope and expectation that this will continue.

Equally we hope that others, particularly those in the helping professions (e.g. therapists, counsellors, social workers and various personnel specialists) will join them, each bringing new interpretations and techniques thereby enriching the approach.

The book is a statement of our 'work in progress' and as such it constitutes a description and analysis of the very recent and the more distant past. In all this we have drawn on our experiences of working together for six years running a range of interpersonal skills training courses, many of them involving personal process work. Some have been for particular companies, others as 'open' programmes at the college; some have had a very specific skill focus (e.g. counselling, consultancy and influencing), others have been a more general exploration of interpersonal skills and relationships. We have also spent a lot of time training interpersonal skills trainers, encouraging and helping them to learn about, experience and practise personal process work.

Writing the book has helped us clarify not only our values and beliefs but also our aims and methods. In addition, the very activity of writing has led us to re-examine from a new perspective our relationships with each other. This has been painful, exciting and joyous. The title 'Unfinished Business', therefore, reflects the nature of personal learning and our recognition that personal process work is a developing approach.

If, through the book, the reader develops or becomes aware of any unfinished business, we should like to hear about it. This could mean for different individuals feelings of curiosity, fear, excitement, pleasure, anger or disagreement.

This book has been written within the wider context of our work at Roffey Park Management College. As an organisation the college is dedicated to the training, development and growth of people within organisations. Many of the college staff have shown this dedication by the support they have given *our* training, development and growth. We are particularly indebted to John Giles, Director, and Robin Evenden, Deputy Director, for giving us encouragement and resources for completing the book. Robin has also given us much useful comment and feedback in the preparation of the book, as has our colleague, Patricia Shaw. We would also like to acknowledge a colleague and friend, Tony Fraser, who worked with us for four of the last six years, for his contribution to our personal and professional development. We are also very grateful to the secretaries at the college for their patience and hard work in typing the book.

Three other groups of people deserve special mention. Firstly, all the participants who have worked with us and who have made this book possible by joining us in taking risks and being willing to explore the consequences. We would particularly like to thank those who gave their permission for us to use the transcripts in Chapter 4. Secondly, there are those teachers, trainers, facilitators and group leaders, too numerous to name, who have offered us challenge, excitement and learning in our own development.

Finally, and most important of all, our wives for being who they are and especially for offering their support and encouragement both in writing this book and in our work as trainers.

Neil Clark   Roffey Park Management College
Keri Phillips   Forest Road
Dave Barker   Horsham
                                    West Sussex RH12 4TD

LIST OF TABLES

INTRODUCTION

The setting

The last thirty-five years have seen the development of a wide range of approaches to interpersonal skills training in a variety of organisations in both the public and private sectors. By 'interpersonal skills training' we mean a planned event intended to help somebody increase his* awareness of himself and his impact on others. This can involve many types of training techniques, methods and philosophies including lectures, role-plays, high trainer control, low trainer control, small groups, large groups, theory, practical work-related exercises, non-work related exercises and so on. (These points are described more fully and put into a context in Chapter 1.)

The extent of interpersonal skills training is considerable and does not appear to have decreased despite adverse economic and social circumstances. This seems to have been due to a number of factors such as:

1   Recognition by many people that the quality of relationships in organisations is a key factor in influencing the quality and productivity of work.
2   Concern about the importance of all human qualities at work,

---

*This book has necessarily been written from male experience (the authors are men and the training groups we work with are, sadly, predominantly men) and this is reflected in a number of ways – not least in our use of the convention of male pronouns throughout the book. We hope that women readers will be able to make connections between our experiences and their own.

including feelings and relationships, in the face of, and in reaction to technological advances and their tendency to 'dehumanise' organisations. This is part of a wider concern in some quarters[1] that mankind has been alienated from his own feelings and environment and is pre-occupied with the intellectual and technological at the expense of the quality of life.

3 The specific demand for employees to be interpersonally as well as technically competent because of harsher economic circumstances and less resources. In other words, there is now less scope for organisations to move technically competent but 'difficult' staff into new jobs. In addition, employees are generally under more pressure to perform at least adequately in all facets of their work.

4 The changed expectations of many employees have led to some lessening of the restrictions on exploring and expressing feelings. Indeed, some organisations have discovered that their effectiveness depends on encouraging this trend (e.g. assertiveness training).

Within this setting there has been increasing usage and development of a particular approach to interpersonal skills training. We have termed this *personal process work*. This has its own distinct philosophy and skills and is essentially a joint activity between a trainer and a trainee where the latter is helped to develop awareness of himself and the ways he makes relationships, with particular attention being paid to underlying meanings and feelings. This work takes place within the context of a training programme of designated length and may proceed to:

1 The development of a wider range of *choices* in handling relationships.
2 *Experiments* in trying out some of these choices.
3 Making *decisions* about what works for them in different situations.

Personal process work can often lead the individual concerned to make a dramatic re-appraisal of himself and the values he has regarding relationships. It could conclude, for example, with the discovery that he can express interest in other people's problems without having to take responsibility for them; or that expressing dislikes does not necessarily lead to alienation; or that the expression of anger can lead to close and collaborative relationships.

The activity called 'personal process work' is concerned with the *processes* of the individual. This means both the feelings, values and motivations that occur *within* that person (e.g. 'I must always win';

'I'm useless'; 'I'm lovable'; 'If people cry I can't cope') and the consequence of these internal dynamics for the *external*, i.e. the behaviour which is manifested whether it be a nuance of non-verbal behaviour (e.g. a slightly raised eyebrow) or a more obvious manifestation; for example, being highly argumentative. The role of the trainer, therefore, in leading somebody in personal process work, can involve the exploration of such aspects as voice tone, facial expression, mismatches between what is said and how it is said, repeated patterns of behaviour, feelings, rules, beliefs etc. There are indeed many entry points and methods available. The primary function of this book is to describe these and the underlying issues.

The authors, based at Roffey Park Management College, have, as trainers, engaged in personal process work with four main areas of activity:

1 A five-day programme based on personal process work. This course, 'Interpersonal Relationships in Organisations' is described in detail in Chapter 4.
2 Programmes concerned with specific skill development, but having a high personal process component.
3 Programmes concerned with introducing trainers to interpersonal skills training and personal process work.
4 Courses designed for specific organisations where personal process work is a minor or major aspect of the programme.

In the light of this experience the authors decided to write a book because personal process work is very different from other forms of training, demanding particular skills and abilities, and sometimes being the subject of much misunderstanding, disagreement and criticism. They also wanted to stand back from their pleasures, disappointments, fears and excitements of recent years to reflect on their experiences and consider the implications for themselves, and others directly or indirectly concerned with interpersonal skills training.

The authors believe that these implications are quite considerable because the skills, values and methods of personal process work are frequently applicable across the whole spectrum of interpersonal skills training and enable the trainer to manage more effectively even those situations where there is negligible emphasis on the participants learning about themselves. For example, an argumentative participant will need to be handled regardless of the context, although obviously the context will determine the method of handling. Individual processes, such as those described above, will be taking place in any training environment and the trainer will probably be more effective if he develops an appreciation of what these processes might be. He can then use this appreciation, whether it be based on knowledge, intuition or both, to decide whether and/or how to intervene, i.e. an intervention intended directly to affect the processes within the individual and the group. Allied to this is the vital awareness which the trainer needs of his own processes in terms of, for example, his feelings or the patterns of his own non-verbal behaviour, or the mismatches between what he says and how he says it.

It has therefore been our aim in this book to put personal process work into a broader setting as the following section describes.

The book

This book develops from a broad exploration of interpersonal skills training (IST) to focus specifically on personal process work and the issues raised for trainers, trainees and organisations.

The first chapter presents an overview of three key training approaches used (thinking, doing and feeling) and the styles involved in each one, including a discussion of their appropriateness and limitations. In addition, the important concept of process is examined in detail. Chapter 2 explores training interventions based on the idea of process and looks at these in the context of the three different approaches already described. Additionally, two important concerns in interpersonal skills training are raised. The first one is handling the 'difficult' course member; the second is the choices available in making process interventions with course members generally, not just the 'difficult' ones. This chapter concludes with a consideration of 'risk' in interpersonal skills training generally and personal process work in particular, looking at issues to do with trainers working as a team (co-training) and highlighting the importance of self-awareness for the trainer. These aspects are indeed themes recurring throughout the book.

Chapter 3 focuses specifically on personal process work, defining it, setting it in the context of its humanistic psychology background, and clarifying its relationship with, and distinction from, the related activity of counselling. Choices between personal process interventions at either the individual or the group level are discussed, together with the role of the trainer in personal process work. As mentioned earlier, in order to illustrate the concept of personal process work in the context of a training programme, the course *Interpersonal Relationships in Organisations (IRO)* is examined in Chapter 4. This takes the form of a review of its nature, aims, history and 'structure'. The all important 'feelings' dimension of the course is highlighted, in part using first person singular to capture the 'here and now' experience of a trainer working on the programme.

Personal process work raises many professional and ethical issues and concerns. These are discussed in Chapter 5, including the problems associated with personal change, the values of personal process work and the limitations of those values, and further consideration of the role and responsibilities of the trainer. This chapter also examines the relationship of personal process work to therapy, a major worry for trainers, trainees and organisations alike.

Chapter 6 looks at the training of trainers, with examples of bodies offering formal services for professional and personal development. This chapter also highlights the demands made on trainers in personal process work and the needs not only for development but also for taking steps to avoid 'burn-out' (i.e. emotional and/or physical exhaustion, normally leading to a loss of creativity and commitment). The book finishes with appendices: two on Transactional Analysis and Gestalt in personal process work (with a minimum of theory to give a broad understanding of their central ideas); and the third appendix outlines some illustrative personal process exercises. There are also a glossary of terms and a booklist.

The readership

In terms of readership, the book first of all provides extensive information on the nature of personal process work and the handling of process issues for those *internal trainers* currently involved, or about to be involved, in interpersonal skills training. These include not only supervisory and management trainers (and those who manage such trainers) but also those involved in public and customer contact work. Relevant areas of their work might include interviewing skills (including appraisal and counselling), communication, leadership and membership skills, influencing, negotiating and assertion skills, supervisory and management styles, team-building, organisation development and personal awareness training. *External trainers* working in the same fields (independent consultants, members of consultancy groups, organisation development specialists, management college staff and academic staff in higher education) will also find the book of relevance. The book will be useful in explaining personal process work to those *personnel staff* who manage interpersonal skills trainers and/or advise managers on the appropriateness of this type of training for employees.

In addition, the book will be of interest to members of other 'helping professions' such as *counsellors, therapists* and *social workers* who are involved in the same educational and learning process. Approaches similar to personal process work are used extensively in many of these professions and in particular by the trainers of such professionals. For example, many social workers attend training events using such personal process-based approaches as Transactional Analysis (TA) and Gestalt. The skills of therapists and counsellors have many parellels with those of trainers in the personal process work area.

Finally, the book will provide, for *managers* and *supervisors* and various organisational *specialists*, insight into the nature and experience of personal process work, based on either their past or future involvement in an interpersonal skills training programme.

The map is not the territory

In writing this book all we can do is provide a rough map of the area, describing our experiences and letting the reader share them. We have sought to explain in a logical way what has been in many ways a meandering journey. Our experiences now make more sense than they did at the time! For us necessity has often been the mother of invention and the particular causes of the success or failure of many an intuitive crisis decision have only become apparent later. So there is an inherent contradiction in attempting to write an analytical, logical and systematic book about relationships, processes and feelings which are, by definition, subjective and idiosyncratic.

With this in mind we encourage the reader to be sceptical so that he can discard, amend and build on what we have done in order that, most importantly of all, he can then operate in ways which make sense and feel right for him. In this way each person can develop his own unique map and work from a position of integration, excitement and curiosity whilst at the same time accepting that there will be times when he is confused, uncertain and lost, perhaps even returning to his starting point. Such journeys, we believe, are rich in learning.

Reference

1 'Work and the Future – technology, world development and jobs in the eighties'. A report from the Industrial Committee of the General Synod Board for Social Responsibility. C.I.O. Publishing, London 1979.

1
INTERPERSONAL SKILLS TRAINING

The whole area of interpersonal skills training can be rather confused and confusing. We are therefore concerned in this chapter to provide the reader with a map which will chart the territory we have in mind and also provide a reference point for the remainder of the book. Our definition of interpersonal skills training (IST) is, 'Any form of training that is designed to help people understand themselves more, learn about how others see them and develop additional choices in how they manage their relationships'.[1] Such a definition clearly covers a wide range of topics and activities in management training, e.g. team-building, group membership and leadership skills, coaching, counselling, negotiating, training, selling, consultancy, assertion and influencing skills, life-planning etc. Thus, within an organisational context, it can deal with such issues as management style, how people relate to authority figures, intergroup conflict, handling relationships with people outside the organisation (e.g. client contacts), attitudes to change, etc. On the assumption that the home environment and atmosphere can have a substantial and often dramatic impact at work and vice versa, then IST can additionally be seen as influencing these areas, with managers on some training programmes considering such questions as: 'What do I want to do with the rest of my life?' 'What can I do to stop taking bad feelings generated at work back to my family?' or 'What can I do to manage and reconcile the conflicting demands of my work and family?'

This wide range of topics and activities involved in IST is matched by an equally wide range of training methods. However, generally these can be categorised as having three significant orientations or approaches: thinking, doing and feeling.

1

THE THINKING APPROACH

Methods used

The thinking approach puts a strong emphasis on people learning through thinking. Typical methods are lectures, films, tape/slide presentations, programmed learning texts and 'structured' discussions. (i.e. discussions led in such a way that the trainer's points emerge). The trainees are given information to think through, discuss, and then decide whether it makes sense to them.

Trainer style and philosophy

With these methods most of the communication is one-way, with the trainer frequently taking over the role of the expert. He knows, or should know, his subject in considerable depth and his main effort is directed towards passing his special knowledge on to the group. As a result of his 'special' position he may also be giving 'right' answers, pointing out where people are wrong and using his authority in an obvious way. Indeed, his authority may well be quite formal and reveal itself through dress (suit and tie for male trainers or a classic cut two-piece in a conservative colour for female trainers), seating arrangements (people sitting in rows, or in a U-shape with name plates) and general space allocation (with the trainer occupying a particularly large amount). Some trainers using the thinking approach do allow the group more freedom to identify and work with answers that are 'right' for them.

The origin and impact of the training need may be quite variable. At one extreme a training need may not really have been identified at all. Rather, somebody, quite possibly unilaterally, decided that it would be a good idea if somebody were brought in, for example, to 'galvanise the sales team'. At the other extreme the participants themselves may have been exerting pressure, e.g. 'You can't expect us to implement this particular item of government legislation unless an expert comes in to tell us all about it'.

A final point to stress here is that the trainer will be taking a 'there and then' orientation i.e. it is highly unlikely that he will encourage the participants to look at their 'here and now' relationships as they sit in the training group. He may well, however, ask people to reflect back on past experiences; those experiences might relate back to the previous day or perhaps the previous twenty years.

Table 1.1
Example of the thinking approach

1 Lecture on motivation based on the work of Maslow, McGregor and Herzberg.

2 Syndicate discussion to consider how the theory relates to the participants' own work experience.

3 Full group review to consider the findings of each syndicate group.

4 Trainer's summary itemising the key points from the session, possibly identifying action which ought to be taken at work in order to increase staff motivation.

Appropriateness and limitations

The thinking approach is likely to have the advantage of fitting in with the organisational culture of the participants. Where the organisation is hierarchical with an emphasis on formal authority, then the trainer, by reflecting this culture, will probably be accepted, i.e. the training method itself is unlikely to provoke anxiety or uncertainty, although there may be some resentment about the training event taking place at all; e.g. the sales force may firmly believe that they do not need to be 'galvanised'. Part of the matching between the thinking approach and organisational culture is also likely to be due to the previous educational experiences of the participants. It is probable that at school or college they will have been expected to fit into a formal system with a teacher or lecturer taking the role of expert. So, the methods associated with the thinking approach will not come as a surprise.

Also, in many instances, it will be quite appropriate for the trainer to take on the role of expert, particularly in dealing with topics where there are right answers. For example, there may be some very clear rights and wrongs on how to fill in an appraisal form or conduct a recruitment interview. Theory can be useful in drawing threads together, and indeed powerful in helping people make sense of themselves and their experience. However, despite the potential for some theory to be quite penetrating, generally the participants will feel safe. Even if the theory directly challenges the participant's values or view of himself, he can find a number of escape routes, for example, by deluding himself that it does not really apply to him, or by conjuring up a stereotype of interpersonal skills trainers (living in ivory towers, being amateur psychologists etc.) or by doing the crossword!

Thus 'safety', a common characteristic of the thinking approach, may work destructively by providing too many escape routes, but equally it can be constructive in terms of helping people to settle down, feel comfortable and be prepared to learn. (The ideas of 'safety' and the closely related one of 'risk' are fundamental areas in IST and will be frequently referred to in this book, both directly and indirectly.)

As a result of the formality of the thinking approach there can be a lack of flexibility (i.e. a need to cover a certain number of items in a limited period of time). Occasionally this can border on the farcical as where, in a tightly structured discussion, the trainer is having to work very hard to extract from the group a particular word or phrase which matches exactly what he has on his next overhead transparency. 'I think what you are really trying to say is . . . '

Associated with this lack of flexibility there may be a considerable degree of dependency in the group, with the participants being swept along by the structure of the programme and/or the charisma of the presenter. Consequently, rather than considering carefully and chewing over what they are told, they may 'swallow whole' the prescribed wisdom and be constantly demanding the right answer. Sometimes this insistent demand for the right answer can be a way in which the group rejects the trainer and his approach; i.e. 'Prove to me that you have a perfect solution for every problem.'

THE DOING APPROACH

Methods used

The doing approach emphasises learning through doing and the acquisition of skills through carrying out practical work. Participants are given tasks to do; e.g. carrying out a role-play which may have been developed from case study material; taking part in an organisational simulation where people may act as marketing manager, personnel officer, trade union official etc.; being involved in an unstructured discussion where relationships in the group may be covered and where there is an opportunity to practise certain communication skills.

An activity which very clearly falls into the doing approach would be where one group of participants is given a problem to solve whilst the remainder observe and give feedback on such issues as leadership, the pattern of communication (i.e. who speaks to whom), the quality of listening, non-verbal behaviour and time management.

Table 1.2
Example of the doing approach

---

1   Everybody is asked to note down *five* criteria for assessing the effectiveness of a work group.

2   The group is split into *task* group and *observer* group. The task group has 20 minutes to agree and put in priority order 5 criteria for assessing group effectiveness. The decision has to be on the basis of *consensus*.

3   The observers each observe one member of the *task* group and also the *task* group generally, using the individual criteria established in 1.

4   After the exercise the *task* group spends 10 minutes assessing its performance using the criteria it developed. Meanwhile the observers prepare to give feedback using their criteria.

5   Full group review of the exercise.

Trainer style and philosophy

As will become clear later the doing approach in many ways occupies a middle road in IST. Consequently the trainer styles can vary considerably. For example, in reviewing the group problem solving exercise referred to earlier, the trainer could take a 'right answers' stance similar to that taken in the thinking approach. He might, in other words, use the exercise to illustrate theoretical points he had already made, generally taking the position, 'It just goes to prove what I said . . . '

Alternatively the review could be handled in a much more open-ended way, encouraging the participants to consider what *they* got out of the exercise, with little, if any, reference to 'the right answer'. This fluidity is also reflected in other aspects of the doing approach.

Role-plays can be made 'lower risk' where participants are asked to play characters vastly different from themselves.[2] (The big escape route for a 'poor' performance here is that the person can say, 'I wouldn't have got myself in that position in the first place', or 'I wasn't comfortable handling it in the way you suggested in the brief'.) The risk level could be increased by the participants acting themselves.

('You had a problem with your boss last week; let's set it up so that somebody in the group role-plays your boss, whilst you play yourself and find a different way of handling this relationship'.)

Also the time focus can be changed either by the trainer and/or the participants. The trainer can take a 'there and then' focus by, for example, encouraging the trainees to reflect on their experiences of group problem solving in the past. Alternatively he may bring it nearer the present by reviewing the problem solving activity which has just taken place; or else he might switch to the 'here and now' by looking at the quality of the relationship between the task group and the observer group as they give and receive feedback. (See Table 1.2.)

As a general rule the more the trainer moves into the 'here and now', the higher the risk level; this is because there are fewer and fewer escape routes. For example, unless it was very dramatic and stressful it is probable that most people would be willing to talk about a mistake they made twenty years ago; they would be less willing to talk about a mistake they made last week; and they will be even less willing to talk about a mistake they made in the exercise half an hour ago.

Reviewing the past provides an easy escape route; it provides the opportunity for people, rightly or wrongly, to say 'I wouldn't do it that way again'; 'I was too young to know any better'; 'The person I was dealing with was totally insensitive', etc. A switch into the here and now confronts them with their current relationships and their ability to face somebody and say, for example, 'I find you totally insensitive', or 'I really like you'.

In the doing approach skills in giving and receiving feedback are very important. They are a key mechanism for learning: trainees learning from trainers and trainers learning from trainees. This latter point is worth noting because, as the training becomes more flexible and participative then the more likely it is that the trainer will be receiving direct feedback about the course. In the thinking approach the trainer may receive some indirect feedback through the glazed or excited expressions on the faces of the group. However, it is uncommon, although not unknown, for a member of the group to stand up and say, 'I think you're talking a load of rubbish'; or, 'What you're saying is really fascinating'. In the doing approach there will be extensive direct feedback to the trainer especially if giving and receiving feedback are skills he wants to develop in the group.

Appropriateness and limitations

A significant advantage of the doing approach is that people are developing skills and have the opportunity to apply in a practical way certain theories or principles; they can then start deciding whether or how these skills can be applied at work. To state the obvious, when it comes to learning there is no real substitute for 'having a go'.

The possible limitations of the doing approach largely revolve around the way the trainer handles the material and the group. For example, trainees can rightly believe they have been cornered into carrying out a task which has been set up simply to prove a particular point; e.g. the group is given such limited resources that it is bound to 'fail'.

Another possible problem is too much or too abrupt switching of the time focus, e.g. looking at relationships in a group exercise, then suddenly looking at work, then some theory, then back to the 'here and now'. There is a real danger of opening up issues and not working them through to some point of satisfaction for the individual trainee and the group. Changing the time focus requires fine judgement; and the skills and factors involved are dealt with later. (See pp. 28-9)

Sometimes the tasks themselves are deliberately non-work related (e.g. sorting playing cards into a particular sequence) and this may increase their chances of rejection by the group. With in-company groups, most especially where there are different levels of hierarchy, the risk level is automatically higher and the trainer will need to bear this in mind when he makes interventions: fears of making a fool of oneself or saying something that will be later used in evidence are greater; confidentiality by all parties will be even more important and will be more difficult to maintain.

THE FEELING APPROACH

Methods used

The feeling approach stresses the importance of feelings as a factor to be explored in IST. The general heading often used for this approach is 'sensitivity training'[3] and this is very much an umbrella term which encompasses a large number of training methods. There are some underlying themes, however, and within these themes different emphases; for example;

1 Non-verbal behaviour: the 'T' group[4] focuses on this as part of a strategy for increasing the group's awareness of behaviour and attitudes in themselves and others. Bioenergetics[5] looks at feelings which may be locked into the body, and the various muscle tensions which may flow from this. The Encounter[6]

method will approach non-verbal behaviour, such as touch, as a way of making contact with others.

2   'Here and now': looking at feelings and relationships as they develop in the 'here and now'.

3   Taking full responsibility for one's life and not blaming others for one's unhappiness and dissatisfaction; linked with this is a belief in the need to be proactive.

Other themes are covered later (see pp. 42–3). This type of training is often called 'unstructured' but in many ways this is misleading. The feeling approach is unstructured in the sense that, in contrast to the thinking and doing approaches, there is unlikely to be a detailed and specific programme. However, even the most open-ended design develops its own structure and should, anyway, have a clearly defined philosophy. It may be an unusual structure, but it is a structure nevertheless. Structure may indeed be more obviously provided in terms of specific exercises, even to the extent of being given sentences for completion.[7]

Trainer style and philosophy

Despite the point we have just made about structure the atmosphere in the group is likely to be informal, indicated through dress (sweaters, jeans, sandals, tee shirts), seating arrangements (people sitting in a circle, perhaps on the floor) and the trainer not obviously having more space than anyone else. Whereas the training with the thinking and doing approaches is likely to have a predetermined and specific focus (possibly linked with behavioural objectives)[8] the feeling approach will almost certainly have wide aims, such as 'increased awareness of self and others'. The participants are likely to be encouraged to be more specific as the course progresses and needs, once identified, (often the hardest part) may well change.

Usually a great deal of responsibility is given to the group and the individuals within it to identify their own learning needs; their reaction to this responsibility is often a learning exercise in its own right. Indeed the whole activity can be seen as one of learning how to learn, including the assuming of responsibility for oneself, one's actions, feelings and one's own future.

Once again explicit feedback will be an important vehicle for learning, but feedback without a task orientation; i.e. the feedback is based on the 'real' relationship, rather than what people did during a problem solving activity or an organisational simulation. The role and attitude of the trainer will inevitably be a key issue that will emerge sooner or later. He will need specific skills in handling the copious amounts of direct and indirect feedback, some of it very negative.

The feeling approach can be very enlightening by focussing on some simple and fundamental issues that the participants may have about relationships (e.g. 'Why do I keep myself at a distance from others?'; 'Why do I put myself down with authority figures?'; 'How do I stop myself expressing warmth?') This enlightenment is enhanced by the 'here and now' time focus. Usually, 'talking about' other people outside the group, or 'what might have been' is discouraged and the point becomes the stark one of 'my relationship with you', 'what I like/dislike about you' or 'what I can give you and you can give me'.

Where such issues are being explored then the centre of attention is the person rather than the manager in his role. The training method then becomes higher risk with the rewards for 'success' and the costs of 'failure' being higher as well.

Table 1.3
Example of the feeling approach

---

1 The group sits in a circle, without tables, so that everyone can see everyone else. The trainer sits in as part of the group.

2 The trainer takes a ruler and initiates proceedings by passing it out to anybody he wants to in the group, whilst giving that person feedback in terms of 'What I like about you is ...; and What I would like you to consider is ...'

3 The receiver of the feedback then passes it on to somebody else, but following the format demonstrated by the trainer.

N.B.   (a)   It is important that the feedback is genuine and says something about the relationship of the two people concerned.

(b)   The trainer may intervene from time to time to check what a person is doing with the feedback they have received – accepting, rejecting, punishing self, feeling good, etc.

Appropriateness and limitations

The feeling approach may constitute something of a culture shock for many managers and organisations, particularly where both have a long tradition of not expressing feelings particularly ones such as fear or anger. With this approach there is little scope for sitting at the back of the room doing a crossword or, as can sometimes happen with the doing approach, going through the motions of a role-play and 'making the right noises'.

This culture shock may work positively or negatively. There is a lot to be said in support of training which either in terms of context or style, challenges organisational and individual norms, or provides a new way of looking at the world. However, this challenge, if too great, can be seen as a threat which leads to a closing of ranks and moves to exclude the 'heretical' trainer. There may ensue a destructive spiral of pressure and resistance: the trainer trying to pressurise the group to see the world in the same way as he does, and the group, with equal energy, resisting, becoming entrenched and reiterating their traditional values and beliefs.

In the feeling approach the trainer will need to be clear on how he establishes and manages a boundary between training and therapy. Since often it is the raw and basic material of relationships which is being explored, domestic problems, (and even issues relating to early childhood), may emerge and need to be dealt with, either in terms of 'working them through' or acting as a reference point for further professional help. For example, in dealing with a problem regarding his relationship with his boss a participant may discover that there are strong similarities between his boss and his father; indeed this may be the source of the problem. It could well be that this person would need to go to a therapist in order to explore his childhood and his subsequent attitude to authority figures. The important ethical considerations concerning training and therapy are dealt with in more detail later (see pp. 103–5).\

The feeling approach may lack specific work application but an assumption is made that because it deals with the 'whole person' there is bound to be a 'knock-on effect' in management skills. For example, if somebody learns how he distances himself in relationships, then it is likely that this learning will have a direct effect on how he manages staff. This adaptation to the work situation can be made so long as, whilst considering feelings, specific skills are also identified and practised during the training.

INTEGRATING THE APPROACHES

So far the thinking, doing and feeling approaches have been largely described as if they were mutually exclusive. However, when seen as parts of a spectrum they then provide a framework for potentially complementary styles and philosophies, enabling the trainer to make a wide range of interventions. Table 1.4 illustrates this, as well as summarising the points made earlier in this chapter.

The effectiveness of the trainer is likely to be increased the more freedom he gives himself to move up and down the spectrum, as

Table 1.4
Integration of approaches

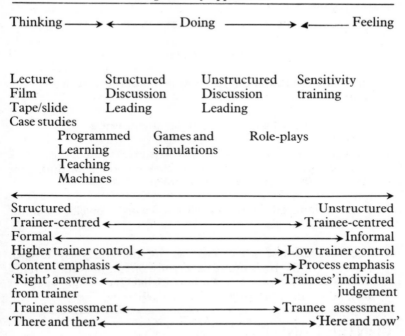

Thinking ⟶ ⟵ —————— Doing ————⟶ ⟵—— Feeling

Lecture	Structured	Unstructured	Sensitivity
Film	Discussion	Discussion	training
Tape/slide	Leading	Leading	
Case studies			
	Programmed	Games and	Role-plays
	Learning	simulations	
	Teaching		
	Machines		

Structured	Unstructured
Trainer-centred ⟵———⟶	Trainee-centred
Formal ⟵———⟶	Informal
Higher trainer control ⟵———⟶	Low trainer control
Content emphasis ⟵———⟶	Process emphasis
'Right' answers ⟵———⟶	Trainees' individual
from trainer	judgement
Trainer assessment ⟵———⟶	Trainee assessment
'There and then' ⟵———⟶	'Here and now'

appropriate, i.e. depending on the needs of the group, the agreement or contract with the client, and his own needs. This is not to say that each training programme should consist of interventions made right across the spectrum. There will be many occasions where, for example, it will make sense to stay firmly lodged in the thinking approach, e.g. where the need requires the conveying of factual information to a large group of people over a short period of time. At the other extreme, for example when two people are clearly engaged in overt conflict with one another, the feelings approach will probably be highly effective, and moving away from the 'here and now' would really be an avoidance of the issue. Such an avoidance could lead the group to reject the trainer and the programme.

What we are proposing is that if the trainer gives himself permission to explore the spectrum, then he may well find new ways of helping himself and others to learn (see Table 1.5). He could break out of some unproductive patterns, e.g. always acting as the expert and being the one who carries the greatest responsibility for the outcome of the training; or believing that people should always be open about their feelings and thus getting into a spiral of pressure and resistance with the group.

Table 1.5
Example of integrating the approaches

(What follows is an outline of some key points during a week long programme)

1   Theory and discussion on the topic of motivation.

2   Organisational simulation with participants, as part of the review, completing questionnaires on their levels of motivation during the exercise and the factors affecting them.

3   Brainstorming groups dealing with real work problems about the motivation of staff.

4   Feedback exercise where members of the group say to each person, 'On the basis of my experience of you this week I think your strengths in motivating others are likely to be . . . ; and your weaknesses in motivating others are likely to be . . .'

CONTENT AND PROCESS

Table 1.4 mentions the words 'content' and 'process'; they are important because managing the content and process dimension will be the basis for managing the spectrum as a whole.

When looking at relationships between people an important distinction can be made between *content* and *process*. Commonly this is referred to as the words, and the music behind the words. More often than not the process level of communication reveals itself non-verbally through tone of voice, eye contact, gestures etc. This is most clearly the case when there is a mismatch or incongruence between the content and process:

> I'm sorry, but (I'm not at all sorry really)
> We'll come back to that later (I don't know how to handle this, let's hope he/she forgets about it)
> Oh, . . . I see (I don't know what on earth you're talking about)
> No, No . . . . I'm fine (I'll make you suffer)
> With all due respect (You're talking a load of rubbish)

Are you sure about that? (I don't believe you)
Why did you do it that way? (You've really made a mess of it!)
Pop into my office for a moment would you please? (I'm going to carpet you!)

The process level within the communication reflects the feelings of the person and it is therefore more powerful than the content. The process level will be the ultimate determinant of the quality and outcome of the communications and the relationship. It is therefore important to be 'tuned in' to the process level of communication in order to exercise choice over the best ways to handle oneself and the other person. Sometimes, for example, people send out a process message outside their awareness (e.g. a brusque manner) which is interpreted by others (rightly or wrongly) as meaning 'Go away!'

This distinction between content and process, together with the importance of 'tuning in' has implications in a wide variety of settings.

For *managers*, whether relating to bosses, colleagues, subordinates or clients, the process dimension will reflect the basis on which fundamental issues such as warmth/distance, conflict/collaboration, dependency, trust, fear, support are established and maintained. At a very simple level it will obviously be important for a manager to recognise that when one of his staff says in a faltering way, 'Oh . . . I think I understand', he may not really, and his lack of understanding could lead to extreme difficulty by the wrong figures being produced, or even physical harm because a machine was not operated properly. The manager will need to deal with this process level communication either *implicitly*, ('I would like you to give me a brief summary of your understanding'), or *explicitly*, ('From the way in which you said that I seriously doubt whether you really do understand. How come you're unwilling to say that you do not understand?')

For *consultants*, whether external or internal, particularly if they are called in at a time of crisis, there will be considerable activity at a process level: fear, resentment, dependency and resistance, not being expressed openly but revealing themselves through tone of voice, innuendoes ('The last consultant we had didn't help us very much, I'm sure you can do better'), coming late to meetings, and so on. The consultant will need to have a repertoire of ways for handling this: *explicitly*, for example, by sharing his perception of the process, ('Judging by your tone of voice you are suspicious of me'); *implicitly* by, for example, offering support without directly mentioning the fear which he believes is beneath the surface.

In both the examples given above the manager and the consultant are making implicit and explicit process interventions.

For *interpersonal skills trainers* the implications are as great if not greater since the majority of their work will revolve around helping others to learn about the process dimension in relationships. In doing this the trainer will probably need to help the trainees move through four stages:

1. Increasing *awareness* of themselves and their impact on others. Feedback will be important here; perhaps feedback from the observers of a problem solving exercise (doing approach), 'here and now' feedback from the trainer and fellow trainees (feeling approach) and perhaps direct feedback from the trainer; 'My assumption from the fact that you are doing the crossword is that you do not want to be here' (thinking approach). The feedback will normally focus mainly on non-verbal communication.

2. This feedback can then be used to develop *choices*, e.g. 'Perhaps when I'm next briefing a group I'll speak more slowly and clearly, rather than trying to hurry up'.

3. The choices then lead to *experiments* where the new behaviour or style is carried out. The experiments can also be used to test what might have been a fairly vague assumption.

4. Finally, a *decision* has to be made about the appropriateness and value of the new behaviour, e.g. 'Does the fact that it worked on the course necessarily mean that I can use this approach with my boss?'

These stages will equally apply to the trainer himself – increasing his awareness of what he does and how he does it; developing new choices and adding to his repertoire of skills; trying new things and making decisions about their appropriateness. In this way the trainer can explore and manage the training spectrum and learn about the different types of process interventions he can make with individuals and groups. This is the subject of the following chapter.

References

1. Phillips K. and Fraser T. *The Management of Interpersonal Skills Training* Gower, Aldershot, 1982.
2. Maier N.R.F., Solem A.R. and Maier A.A. *The Role-Play Technique – a handbook for management and leadership practice.* University Associates, La Jolla, 1975.
3. Seashore C. 'What is Sensitivity Training?' *Reading Book for Human Relations Training* Porter L. and Mohr B. (eds) NTL Institute, Arlington, 1982.

4   Smith P.B. 'The 'T' Group Approach' from *Improving Interpersonal Relations – some approaches to social skill training*, Cooper C. (ed) Gower, Aldershot, 1981.
5   Lowen A. *Bioenergetics*, Penguin, Harmondsworth, 1975.
6   Schutz W. *Joy* Penguin, Harmondsworth, 1967.
7   Pfeiffer, J.W. and Jones J.E.. See an exercise called 'Dyadic Encounter', *A Handbook of Structured Experiences for Human Relations Training Vol. I Revised* University Associates, San Diego, 1969.
8   Gronlund N.E. *Stating Objectives for Classroom Instruction* Collier-Macmillan, London, 1978.

2
PROCESS
INTERVENTIONS

Chapter 1 provided an overview of interpersonal skills training, including reference to a spectrum which the trainer can use and explore to increase his range of options in carrying out his work. Our concluding point concerned 'content' and 'process'. In this chapter we want to look in more detail at how content and process relate to the various approaches already described and also the implications for the trainer in terms of the process interventions he might make.

In the context of training our working definition of a *process intervention* is:

> Any intervention made by the trainer specifically to affect directly:
> 1 The quality and nature of the relationships within the group;
> 2 The feelings, behaviour, attitudes of the individual;
> 3 The relationships between himself and the group, or an individual within it.

This definition will have different applications and consequences according to the orientation of the training, and what follows is a consideration of these points and how they relate to the thinking, doing and feeling approaches.

PROCESS INTERVENTIONS AND THE THINKING APPROACH

Even where the training is firmly based in the thinking approach the trainer will be making process interventions. He will be doing things to affect his relationship with the group, for example by the way in which he dresses, by the furniture arrangements and through his general training style. He is making a non-verbal statement about how he sees himself and inviting or demanding that others relate to him in a particular way.

Many of his process interventions, as in the examples above, will be *implicit* where, through dress etc., he is sending such messages as 'I want you to treat me formally, but we can have a laugh from time to time', or, 'I'm here to control the discussion and I want you to contribute only when I say so'. Our definition of an *implicit process intervention* is therefore:

A considered attempt by the trainer covertly to affect:
1 The quality and nature of relationships within the group;
2 The feelings, behaviour, attitudes of the individual;
3 The relationships between himself and the group, or an individual within it.

In the light of what he knows or imagines about the group, perhaps using information gleaned during the identification of the training need, the trainer will be faced with decisions about whether, how and how far to meet their expectations. The participants may come expecting to be told what they need to know, and that the trainer will do all the teaching. The trainer could make an implicit process intervention challenging this assumption by putting people into small discussion groups, thereby clearly stating (albeit implicitly), 'You can learn from each other as well as from me'.

The trainer will need to do his best to make sure that his communication with the group is congruent at the levels of content and process. Some examples of incongruence are:

'I want you to feel free to contribute' (. . . and yet not allowing time or space for anybody else to speak).
'I want to create a relaxed and informal atmosphere' (. . . and yet acting in a formal and tense way).

This congruence between content and process should also extend to whatever rules or principles the trainer wants to convey to the group. There is, for example, an inherent contradiction between 'selling' the values of collaboration and then deliberately stimulating intergroup conflict (unless it is to prove a particular training point); or stressing the importance of listening and then patently not doing so.

It is valuable therefore for the trainer not only to have *content* aims in terms of what he would like the trainees to learn, but also *process* aims in terms of the type of group atmosphere he would like to have and the types of intervention he is likely to need to make in order to contribute to that atmosphere. For example, the trainer may be running a course on how to complete annual appraisal forms, including an examination of the dangers of stereotyping. If he wants people to examine their own stereotypes then that will require quite a fair degree of trust and he will have to find ways of contributing to that trust by sharing some things about himself, (e.g. mention his past or present stereotypes and their consequences for him) as well as being willing to listen and check his understanding.

The vast majority of the process interventions with the thinking approach will be implicit. However, there may be some explicit process interventions, particularly when things start to go wrong.

Pursuing the example of the appraisal form training, it may be that one of the trainees is being difficult, perhaps by being argumentative. There could be many reasons for such an attitude (resentment at being on the course, bad feelings about training generally, a belief that promotion prospects had suffered in the past because of the appraisal system etc.) The trainer's first choice would probably be to handle it at an *implicit* level.

Trainee: You're telling us to be aware of our stereotypes, but this just sounds like amateur psychology to me. (You're talking a load of rubbish).

Trainer: Well, I still think it's important for people to be aware of their prejudices and the impact these may have on the assessment of people's abilities. (I'm not going to accept being put down by you)

Trainee: But surely it's impossible for somebody to be aware of all their prejudices (I'm still out to get you)

Trainer: Yes, but it's a matter of degree. The more aware you are of your prejudices, the greater your chances of being fair. Certainly if you think I'm showing any prejudices this week I'd be glad if you pointed them out to me. (I'm still not accepting your 'put down', I don't want to spend the whole course fighting you. Let's work together).

Obviously there are many ways of handling such an individual through implicit process interventions. However, a totally different route would be to make *explicit* process interventions.

Trainer: You seem angry with me, what's that about? I don't want us to fight all week, how can we work together?
Are you really, underneath it all, saying that I'm talking a load of rubbish? If you are then I'd like you to say so then I'll know where I stand with you.
It seems as if nothing I can say will make you change your mind.

Our definition of an *explicit process intervention* is therefore:

> A considered and overt attempt by the trainer to help the individual increase his awareness of himself and the quality of his relationships, particularly those within the group. This might include exploring the nature of the relationship between the individual and the trainer.

These explicit process interventions might be made in front of the group, but that is likely to be a higher risk where the trainer and the trainee may feel that their credibility is at stake. The process issue may then assume such proportions as to push the content material to one side. This is not necessarily a bad thing however. For example, the argumentative person may perhaps be a spokesperson for the group where in fact all of them doubt the validity of the training. If this is the case it will in most instances make more sense to try to bring their scepticism to the surface where it can be explored (even at the expense of the published programme) rather than to 'plough on regardless', pretending in the face of all the evidence that everything is really going alright.

PROCESS INTERVENTIONS AND THE DOING APPROACH

With the doing approach there is likely to be a shift towards making a greater number of explicit process interventions. There are a number of reasons for this. Firstly, it is probable that 'process' will be dealt with as a topic within the course material. Whether the training is concerned with interviewing, group problem solving or leadership styles, the participants will probably be asked *how* they organised themselves, what they felt, what types of non-verbal behaviour were evident etc. As a result people are likely to be much more aware of the process levels within the group and between the group and the trainer. The power and effectiveness of the trainer will largely rest on his noticing and working with this awareness of process. To take a clear example: it may be that the trainer has mentioned how the phrase 'with all due respect' can often mean, 'without any respect at all'. If a course member in asking a question uses this phrase then the trainer will need to make some acknowledgement of this, perhaps through teasing or checking out what the trainee really wants to say, or almost doing anything to make it clear that he had noticed this process comment. Similarly, it would be important to pick up 'phoney' questions, i.e. questions which are hiding statements ('Do you really mean to say that . . . ?')

A second reason why greater use is likely to be made of explicit process interventions in the doing approach is that the size of the group will probably be smaller, and people will get to know each other better. There is likely to be a more supportive atmosphere for looking at the 'real' meanings behind the words. Closely linked to this is the fact that because people will be more at risk, through perhaps having to perform on closed-circuit television, their feelings, such as fear and excitement, will be much nearer the surface and consequently more obvious and available for exploration.

A final reason concerns the time focus of the training. Whereas the thinking approach is largely 'there and then', and the feeling approach is 'here and now', the doing approach is a mixture – the 'there and then' often referring to the immediate past of a training exercise, and the 'here and now' referring to the quality of relationships in the group.

A common general format for this type of training is as follows:

1 Brief theory input e.g. on effective decision making in groups.
2 Practical work with half the group being given a problem to solve and the other half acting as observers.
3 Reviewing the activity (perhaps with the aid of television) with the problem solving group reflecting on their experience and receiving feedback from the trainer and the observers.
4 Summarising theory which then quite possibly leads onto another practical exercise.

At the third stage of this format there are several opportunities for making explicit process interventions including, 'What were your feelings at that time?'; 'In looking at that replay how would you describe your tone of voice?'; 'Have you had feedback like this before?'; 'What are you doing now with the feedback you are receiving?'

With the doing approach there will also be a need for implicit process interventions, most of them intended to create an atmosphere of trust where people feel free to experiment and take risks. For example, somebody may feel scared about taking part in a role-play; so scared perhaps that it would be unhelpful to focus explicitly on his fear. The trainer could make implicit process interventions by encouraging the person to choose somebody to work with in preparing for the role-play; offering himself as a resource; establishing a rule that any item of negative feedback must be accompanied by a positive one. All these interventions convey the message, 'You don't have to be scared, you can ask for help and I'm concerned that nobody is given more feedback than they can cope with'.

In handling difficult course members there may be a need for a mixture of implicit and explicit process interventions. For example, somebody who sits quietly saying and doing as little as possible could be handled in a wide variety of ways at a process level:

1 Put him in the same syndicate group as somebody who is quiet, supportive and listens well (implicit)
2 Offer encouragement when they do or say anything (implicit)
3 Talk to the person out of session: (a) about things generally (implicit)
   (b) about how they are in the group (explicit)
4 Make a general comment to the group about the need for contributions (implicit)
5 Have an open review session for talking about feelings, frustrations, giving feedback etc. (implicit and explicit)

PROCESS INTERVENTIONS AND THE FEELING APPROACH

Here there is an emphasis on explicit process interventions. This is because, more often than not, the aim of the training is to treat process as content; the task of the group is to examine its own process. Therefore, the trainer will be making interventions to help people look at what is happening in the 'here and now'. As part of his general strategy of raising awareness he will be encouraging others to do the same and to make explicit process interventions with each other.

Some of the explicit process interventions the trainer might make are:

My interpretation of your tapping foot is . . .
How do you feel about what Fred just said?
I don't like it when you . . .
I like the fact that you . . .
My perception of you as a group is . . .
I want feedback from you.
What do you really want me to do?

The 'difficult course member' will be legitimate subject matter for the course. Dealing with him explicitly will not be a diversion away from the real purpose of the training as it *might* be with the thinking and doing approaches. In the feeling approach the difficult course member might be the person who repeatedly minimises his feelings. He might say 'I'm a little bit annoyed about what is happening here'. A number of explicit process interventions could flow from this:

Exaggerate that feeling of annoyance.
With whom are you annoyed?
Focus on each person in the group and let them know

what it is about them that annoys you.
Who in the group are you annoyed with most?
Who in the group are you annoyed with least?
Draw a picture which represents your annoyance.
Where in your body is your annoyance?

A substantial source of implicit process interventions in the feeling approach comes from the behaviour modelled by the trainer depending on his willingness to express his feelings, to give and receive feedback and to offer support and confrontation.

In the remainder of this chapter we want to give detailed consideration to 'difficult course members' and the different styles of explicit process interventions. Before doing that, however, a summary, given in Table 2.1, outlines the points which have been made so far.

Table 2.1
Summary of approaches

Thinking approach	*Doing approach*	*Feeling approach*
Emphasis on content and implicit process interventions.	Balanced emphasis on content and process.	Emphasis on process, i.e. process is treated as content.
Occasionally explicit process interventions will be made, but often these will be out of session, e.g. in handling difficult course members.	Balance between implicit and explicit process interventions. Most of the explicit process interventions will probably be made out of session.	Emphasis on explicit process interventions.

DIFFICULT COURSE MEMBERS

Several times the phrase 'difficult course member' has been used and indeed it will be used again later in the text. Since the difficult course member represents an obvious area for the application of process interventions, both explicit and implicit, we want to expand further on this topic.

Certainly what constitutes a difficult course member will vary from trainer to trainer. One trainer might have difficulties with 'aggressive' people, another with 'passive people', another with 'argumentative people' and so on. It is quite likely that each trainer has a 'bête noire', a particular type of individual who causes problems, most probably by 'hooking' some vulnerability within him. An important part of self-awareness (see pp. 35–6) is certainly for the trainer to be clear about the types of people with whom he has particular difficulty.

The other important aspect is that, since there are always two sides to a relationship, then the difficulty may be as much, if not more, to do with the trainer as the trainee. Without realising it both may be acting in a destructively collusive way. An example is where the trainer has a general belief that, 'there is always a difficult bugger in the group and I must put him in his place'; and a trainee believes that 'authority figures are there to be fought with'. A probable consequence of these two meeting is that they will spend the whole course fighting and come away from the exchange with their beliefs confirmed.

However, putting to one side the possible responsibility of the trainer, we would define a difficult course member as *somebody who, with or without awareness, blocks his own learning and/or the learning of others*.

The range of options which the trainer has to deal with this person will depend on a number of considerations:

How much of a problem is this person?

How much time might I need to spend on him if I decide to confront him? Would this be at the expense of the course objectives?

What would be an appropriate intervention in terms of the style and approach of the training?

Can I use others in the group as a resource, and not get into scape-goating?

Why am I making this person so important to me?

With these factors in mind then the trainer can move in a number of directions which, in the order below, roughly constitute a move from low risk to high risk. (For a fuller discussion on 'risk' see pp. 33–4)

1 Ignore the behaviour – particularly at the start of a programme where individuals are likely to resort to defensive patterns of behaviour in order to manage their uncertainty. By ignoring the behaviour the trainer allows the individual time and space to build whatever support is required.

2 Content level – make contact with the individual at content level and avoid explicit process interventions, e.g. 'I accept your right to your point of view but I do disagree with you' (use with somebody who is being argumentative).

3 Offer appreciation to the person for appropriate behaviour – say, 'Thank you for that clear and concise point' to somebody who has previously been over-elaborating.

4 Invite other group members to join in – provide an opportunity for the individual to test out his reality, or point of view, with others, e.g. 'Alright, what do the rest of you

think about this?' When doing this it is important to avoid scape-goating and/or exerting too much pressure.

5 Implicit confrontation – by the trainer modelling more open forms of behaviour; by appreciating others in the group for more open forms of behaviour; by introducing theory which describes what the trainer sees as the problem behaviour.

6 Outside session – spend time with the individual outside training sessions to check out his difficulties and/or to confront his behaviour.

7 Invite the individual to explore his behaviour – he will respond to the invitation if he is aware of some level of personal dissatisfaction with what he is doing.

8 Invite the individual to identify other options for himself – ask him if he can find other ways for him to be in the group.

9 Invite other members of the group to give feedback on how they see the relationship between the trainer and the 'difficult course member'.

10 Give permission – give the person permission to behave in that way – 'It's alright with me if you behave like that'.

11 Explicit confrontation – the trainer confronts the individual's behaviour by
   (a) straight feedback – My perception of you is . . .
   (b) invitation to do more – You can learn more about this behaviour by doing more of it (see also p. 151.)
   (c) disapproval – I don't like you when . . .

Below are some more examples of explicit confrontations, related to some 'typical' difficult course members.

Course member

1 *Mr Nice Guy*
Has strong need to be nice to everyone; usually avoids open conflict and generally refuses to discriminate between relationships.

Possible explicit confrontations

(a) I don't like you when you are so nice to me. I don't feel privileged.

(b) I want you to tell me one thing you don't like about me.

(c) I want you to rate people in the room on a 1–10 scale. Those you dislike score 1, those you really like score 10.

(d) Who told you that you

have to be nice to people?

(e) I want you to start each sentence with 'Mr Nice Guy says . . .

(f) The way to get closer to me is to be nasty.

(h) Pay attention to his slightest expression of nastiness (often non-verbal behaviour) and focus him on the behaviour.

2 *Wallflower*

Says and does as little as possible. May give non-verbal signals that he wants someone to rescue him. May play 'Discover me'. (i.e. works from an implicit position of 'I am *very* interesting and it's up to you to discover how interesting I am').

(a) What are you thinking/feeling now?

(b) What are you doing here?

(c) What have you learnt for yourself?

(d) I think you are wasting your time.

(e) What do you do when you're silent?

(f) I forbid you to speak.

(g) Ask him to say/do something.

(h) What do you want from me?

3 *Stupid*

Keeps putting himself down with statements such as 'You may think I'm stupid but . . .'

(a) Yes . . . you're stupid!

(b) Who told you that you were stupid?

(c) On a 1–10 scale I would give you a six for stupidity. How can you score a 10?

(d) What do you get out of being stupid?

(e) You must be very clever to be that stupid!

(f) I want you to be really stupid now.

4 *Persecutor*

Spends most of his time putting others down.

(a) What do you get out of persecuting me/him?

(b) I feel hurt/angry when you persecute me.

(c) How do you persecute yourself?

(d) I don't like you when you persecute.

(e) Got me again . . . I feel really devastated (heavy irony).

(f) Stop it!

(g) What are you scared of now?

5 *Victim*
Spends most of his time putting himself down and/or goes out of his way to attract persecutors.

(a) When you play victim I want to persecute you.

(b) What do you get out of being a victim?

(c) I want you to tell me how pathetic you are.

(d) I guess you must be feeling very bad. (neutral tones)

(e) Describe yourself to me.

(f) Encourage/invite him to put his criticisms out on others.

5 *Rescuer*
Leaps to the defence/aid of others whether they need rescuing or not. Often will say that they are thinking/feeling same as their 'victims'

(a) There you go again.

(b) What do you feel when you rescue?

(c) Tell me why he needs rescuing?

(d) Who do you want to persecute?

(e) Who told you that you have to rescue others?

(f) Who are you really rescuing?

7 *Mr Wood*
Says he has no feelings – will often describe himself and others as neutral.

(a) What would happen if you had a feeling?

(b) I want you to imagine feeling sad/angry/happy . . . what would you look like?

(c) Close your eyes and imagine yourself as a block of wood . . . describe yourself, (or confront in the same way any image he uses about himself).

(d) When did you learn to hide your feelings?

(e) How do you stop your feelings?

(f) Pick up and confront any non-verbal signal.

8 The Interrupter

Habitually interrupts conversations, particularly those which are emotional and/or focus on conflict. Ostensibly interrupts to clarify/understand/explain etc.

(a) How is this important to you?

(b) What is your feedback to me/him/the group?

(c) Shut-up! I'll come to you later.

(d) What are you thinking/ feeling now?

(e) What are the consequences for you when you interrupt like this?

9 The Intellectual

Spends all his time 'intellectualising' his experience. Often slots people into models/ categories.

(a) Most of the strategies outlined for 'Mr. Wood' can be used.

(b) Tell me what you now understand about yourself and others as a result of this week?

(c) I'm interested in your interpretations. I would like you to share them.

(d) Go round the room and tell each person what category you have put them in.

(e) Ask him to make contact with someone without talking.

10 Hurry up

Does everything at a gallop. Talks fast, taps, fidgets. Often expresses irritation at what he considers is a slow pace.

(a) Focus on the non-verbal behaviour – get him to identify with his experience and/or exaggerate it (e.g.talk faster)

(b) Tell him to speed up.

(c) Tell him to slow down.

(d) What would happen to

you if you slowed down?

(e)   Give yourself permission
      to slow down.

PROCESS INTERVENTION STYLES[1]

With this background in mind it is appropriate to look at the styles
and options which the trainer has open to him. The model below is not
intended to cover all the options, nor are the dimensions mutually
exlusive, but it does represent the factors which we have found most
useful and important in our work.

1   There and then ◄————————► Here and now
   Example
          Were you aware of your tone   Pay attention to your tone of
          of voice at that time?   voice now.

Discussion

Time focus has already been mentioned several times as being
important. 'There and then' interventions would commonly be made
when reviewing an activity (role-play, problem solving exercise etc.)
A 'here and now' intervention is a higher risk choice, particularly if it
constitutes a move away from referring to the person in a role, to
looking at the person in real life. This sort of switch can be particularly
powerful where the person is demonstrating in the 'here and now' the
behaviour or attitude which was previously being discussed in the
'there and then' (e.g. if the person seemed inattentive in the interview
– breaking eye contact, not listening – and that is how they appear to
be during the review of the interview). The appropriateness and
productiveness of a move in the 'here and now' will vary considerably.
In one instance it could be that there is a lot of support and trust in the
group and this could lead the particular trainee to go a long way in
exploring for example, his inattentiveness. In other circumstances it
could be that the group is generally dismissive of the training
believing, rightly or wrongly, that they are not learning anything. The
trainer, by switching into the 'here and now' is increasing the risks,
challenging individuals and the group to look at their attitudes.

More often than not any excursion into the 'here and now' will
require more than a one-off intervention; the trainer will have to be
willing to follow through on his needs, interests and concerns.

2   Directive ◄————————————► Non-directive
   Examples
          I want you to . . .   What do you want to do?

Discussion

As a rough generalisation explicit directive process interventions will be made most in the doing approach. Here the trainer is setting up a series of activities, has some specific learning points to make, and will direct the attention of the group to them. In the feeling approach the interventions will tend to be non-directive, thus reflecting the greater responsibility which individuals and the group are expected to assume for their own learning. There will, however, be occasions where it is appropriate to make directive comments in the feeling approach, particularly in terms of offering protection. (See p. 34.) For example, with somebody who is constantly putting themselves down and focusing on their 'bad' points:

I want you to ask each person in the group what they like about you.

I want you to list all your negative qualities no matter how small. (This is an example of getting a person to exaggerate a particular behaviour, as a way of learning more about it – see p. 151).

I want you to draw a picture which represents how you see yourself in relation to this group.

3   Interpretative ←————————→ Non-interpretative
Example

You seem to be unhappy   What are you doing?
about what I just said.

Discussion

Interpretative interventions will probably be made more in the doing approach, where there is a greater amount of 'labelling' taking place, possibly related to some theoretical model e.g. 'You seemed to be very concerned that everyone agreed with your decision and as a result you did not achieve the task'. Where interpretative interventions are made in the feeling approach they will probably be clearly 'flagged' as such e.g. 'I'm not sure, but my interpretation of what you're doing is . . . '
The tentativeness is important because one of the principles of the feeling appproach is that one can never *really know* what is going on inside people, one can only guess through the interpretation of the behaviour which is manifested. Non-interpretative interventions are used most particularly in the feeling approach and it is this move away from the interpretative which trainers often find difficult. This is especially the case where they are working towards modifying their style to cover not only the doing approach but also to include some facets of the feeling approach.

4   Evaluative ◄———————————————► Descriptive
   Example
      You   are   over-elaborating   Notice how nobody has said
      your point.   anything during the last five
                                              minutes.

Discussion

In the doing approach the trainer will probably be expected to take a judgemental role. A probable consequence of relying heavily on evaluative process interventions is that it may 'feed' dependency in the group with trainees becoming unwilling to make their own assessments of what they are doing and its effectiveness. Alternatively, over-reliance on descriptive interventions can lead to frustration in the group, with the trainees not knowing where they stand because the trainer is unwilling to make a clear statement of his views. (This parallels a lament of subordinates who want to know their boss's standards of performance. This anger and frustration flowing from this management style can equal that generated by a highly autocratic and judgemental style.)

   In the feeling approach descriptive interventions have an important role to play in encouraging a clear distinction to be made between observation and subsequent evaluation and/or interpretation. Communication between people can be adversely affected by the lumping together of description and evaluation/interpretation. A simple example is where somebody comes into work late and his boss immediately tells him off assuming that it is because of insolence or laziness rather than a transport delay.

5   Negative ◄———————————————► Positive
   Example
      I don't like you when . . .   I like you when . . .

Discussion

The trainer will be faced with many decisions about whether/how to give negative and/or positive feedback. There are obvious dangers in taking an extreme position. If the trainer always gives negative feedback then the group may well feel victimised, rebel, and end up 'getting their own back'. Similarly, if the trainer is unwilling to give negative feedback he may appear to be inauthentic. The trainees may even do things deliberately wrong in order to provoke the trainer into saying something negative.

Culture and expectations can also be important for the trainer to take into account on this particular aspect of style. The organisational culture of the participants may be one where little positive feedback is given and where there is a general unwritten policy of 'no news is good news'. There may well be a mistrust of positive feedback and any charge of lack of authenticity will be much more to do with the group than the trainer. This could be an issue on which the trainer needs to confront the group directly, making clear his values and beliefs, whilst inviting an exchange of views.

6   Cathartic ◄─────────────────────► Non-cathartic
    Example
        It's O.K. to cry here.   Diverting attention.

Discussion

This discussion concerns what, if anything, the trainer does to encourage emotional release. An underlying assumption here is that the trainer will not, indeed cannot, make people get angry or feel sad etc., but that the training may provide a focus where perhaps months or even years of accumulated feelings come to the surface and will need to be dealt with, directly or indirectly. With the feeling approach this is fairly likely to happen and will be a regular, though not frequent, occurrence. Since the basic philosophy of the training is to do with expressing feelings it will be necessary to make cathartic interventions from time to time. This does *not* mean making somebody cry or express their anger, but rather offering them support in doing this by, for example, giving permission (see pp. 34). To divert attention from these feelings as they first bubble up would probably be seen as incongruent.

In the doing approach it may, however, make sense to divert attention: if on a skills-based programme somebody starts to cry because he put up a 'poor performance' on television then in order to offer that person protection the trainer may suggest a break or invite the person to raise his concerns out of session. Obviously this is a fine point of judgement. Much depends on the nature of the contract, the atmosphere in the group (is it supportive?) and the trainer's guess about whether the root cause of the distress is 'small' or 'large'. If the cause of the crying is simply the poor performance then probably the catharsis will be fairly short and the person will feel reasonably content discussing this in front of the group. At the other extreme, if the cause of the crying is much deeper rooted, concerning 'life issues', then the catharsis might well be a long one, perhaps involving discussion of deeply personal issues which, after the event, the person might have been unhappy to have opened up in front of the group.

7   Sharing feelings ◄————————► Not sharing feelings
   Example
      I'm angry with you   Silence/diverting attention

Discussion

An interesting concern for trainers is whether/how to express feelings, and if so, which ones. In some instances the answer seems obvious. If in making a presentation to a large group of people over a short period of time (i.e. firmly in the thinking approach) the speaker admits to feeling scared and vulnerable then it will at best be pointless: there will be little scope for the audience to offer support, it is unlikely to help in the achievement of the training aims, and at worst it will undermine his credibility with the group since it challenges their expectation that 'experts are not supposed to be scared and vulnerable'. In this setting there is little if any scope for 'working through' the trainer's comments; by making such a comment the trainer does not help the group and he probably does not help himself.

In the feeling approach the situation is very different and the trainer's credibility may actually rest on his expressing feelings, i.e. modelling the behaviour he expects of others. This does not mean expressing every feeling at every time it occurs. This would be a nonsense since it would deny time and space to others and equally it would be unfair and unrealistic to expect a running commentary from others.

Table 2.2 summarises the *general* relationship between the overview model and process interventions.

Table 2.2
Overview model and process interventions

Thinking	Doing	Feeling
There and then ◄————————►		Here and now
Directive ◄————————►		Non-directive
Interpretative ◄————————►		Non-interpretative
Evaluative ◄————————►		Descriptive
Positive (Negative) ◄————————►		Positive *and* Negative

Table 2.2 continued

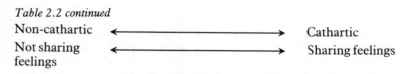

| Non-cathartic | ←——————————→ | Cathartic |
| Not sharing feelings | ←——————————→ | Sharing feelings |

As can be seen, the two examples of implicit process interventions (i.e. non-cathartic and not sharing feelings) are likely to be more in evidence at the thinking end of the training spectrum. This reflects part of the thinking style where the trainer is unlikely to raise and explore overtly his relationship with the group.

FURTHER CONSIDERATIONS

Risk

Several times already in this book the word 'risk' has been mentioned. In the final analysis this is a subjective experience and what is felt as a high risk exercise by one person may seem to be the complete opposite to another. Having said that, there are within the content of an IST programme a number of activities which are likely to stimulate an increased sense of risk:

1   Learning a new skill (which involves doing something different); understanding something new, or experiencing new feelings.
2   Saying something which the person believes may upset someone.
3   Doing something instead of talking or thinking about it.
4   Acknowledging ignorance or a feeling of inadequacy.
5   Finding that a particular behaviour no longer works, in the sense of achieving a certain outcome (e.g. crying no longer gets sympathy).
6   Finding that a particular behaviour or attitude (and by extension a particular way of being in the world) is challenged by others.
7   Observing others behaving in ways that seem strange and bewildering.

Risk can bring with it a sense of excitement, particularly in terms of exploring new areas and this indeed is the basis of learning. On the other hand, where the risk experienced is too great and the person feels that he lacks the internal and/or external resources to cope then he is likely to block out the opportunities for learning. This blocking can take place in many ways: withdrawal, blind reiteration of 'old' values, suspicion, rejection of the group or the trainer or the course material and becoming passive.

Although ultimately it is up to the trainee whether he is going to take a 'positive' or 'negative' attitude to risk, the trainer carries a share of the responsibility. In training design terms this means that the more the trainer moves across the spectrum towards the feeling approach, the greater the chances of the trainee feeling at risk; this is because there is a greater chance of his way of looking at the world being challenged: there are fewer escape routes. If the trainer seeks to increase the risk level then he will need to pay increasing attention to the permission and protection[2] he offers the group.

In broad terms permission, expressed directly or indirectly, says to the group, 'It's alright to go exploring, to try something different and enjoy the excitement'. Protection means the trainer, once again directly or indirectly, indicating that he will act as a 'back-stop; in other words saying to the group, 'I'll do my best to make sure that you do not come to any physical or emotional harm'. Permission and protection can be expressed as a simple diagram. (See Figure 2.1.)

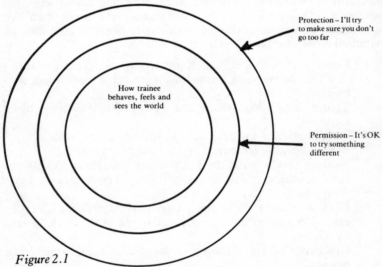

Figure 2.1

The trainer can offer permission in various ways; ranging from explicit statements, through the briefing for exercises, asking people what they got from certain activities, review sessions, to modelling. Protection can come from the contract which is drawn up in the first place, expressing the aims and nature of the training; the early statements from the trainers expressing the ground rules for the course, staying close to the group or particular individuals who have had a difficult time and setting very clear limits for an exercise.

Co-training

In the previous chapter we mentioned incongruence; this was in the context of the trainer taking care that he does not send one message at a content level and a contradictory message at a process level. The need for congruence also applies to the joint training approach where co-training is involved. This is important in a number of respects.

In terms of the overview model it would be unwise and, indeed, dangerous for one trainer to maintain a largely 'thinking' orientation with the group and his colleague to maintain a largely 'feeling' – based approach. In the face of this inconsistency the degree of risk experienced by the group would probably be too high and, as a consequence, they would start resisting in some of the ways referred to above, such as aggression or passivity.

Another way of looking at this issue is to see it in terms of a need for consistency in the permission and protection which is offered to the group. Such offers will be more potent when consistent and consequently are more likely to be accepted. We are not suggesting that the trainers should always be in total agreement in what they say to the group and how they say it, but they should be broadly complementary. The strength of the training could then, for example, lie in the ability of one trainer to challenge and confront, whilst the other is able to be supportive. Having said that the trainers should not get locked into a pattern whereby the supportive trainer never confronts and the confronting trainer never supports. If this does happen then there is a possibility of a good-Daddy, bad-Daddy dynamic being set up with one trainer getting all the appreciations and the other trainer getting all the negative feedback.

Allied to this is the need for the trainers to appreciate the nature of their relationship with each other, especially at a process level. Their effectiveness as a team when making process interventions will be dramatically reduced if they are not aware of their own interaction with each other. For example, if one of the trainers takes a one-down position with regard to his colleague then as a team they will be less effective in dealing with one-down people in the group. (Further aspects of co-training are described on pp. 49–50.)

Self-awareness

What has just been said about the training team also applies to the individual trainer. The more deeply that the trainer becomes involved in IST, especially making process interventions, then the greater the need for him to be aware of his own process – his strengths and vulnerabilities, how he can get 'hooked' into a collusive process, for example by fighting or smothering. This is not to say that the trainer could or should have total self-knowledge (this would be impossible; learning about oneself is a life-time's occupation), but that the trainer should have a reasonable idea of what he is like as a person, and how he appears to others. The trainer will be better able to offer permission and protection to others if he knows how to offer permission and protection to himself by having a sound knowledge of his area of competence.

Obviously the trainer, like the trainee, goes through experimentation and risk taking in order to learn and, at the same time, he will benefit from setting himself limits and exploring gradually. One way of doing this, in terms of the training spectrum, would be to introduce one or two higher risk exercises such as asking people to generate their own role-play material rather than giving them scripted characters to play. There are many ways in which the trainer can help himself to learn, help others, and also maintain his excitement without harming himself or others.

The issue of self-awareness is closely related to the idea of self-development; this means the trainer pursuing his own learning, probably in a variety of ways. This area is covered much more extensively in Chapter 6.

CONCLUSION,

In this chapter we have considered and described process interventions and how they relate to the thinking, doing and feeling approaches. We have emphasised explicit process interventions and these have a particular application in one of the feeling-based approaches known as a personal process work. The detail of personal process work is described in the next chapter and, indeed, the rest of the book describes and explores issues related to this aspect of training and personal learning. Our experience has been that a good understanding of personal process work, where explicit process interventions are made in a highly concentrated way, can help trainers expand their repertoire of process interventions across the training spectrum.

References

1 Heron, John *Dimensions of Facilitator Style*, University of London, 1977.
2 James, M. et al. *Techniques in Transactional Analysis*, Addison Wesley, 1977.

3
PERSONAL PROCESS WORK

In the last chapter we looked at explicit process intervention styles and, generally, how the trainer may use them in the context of the thinking, doing and feeling approaches to IST. In this chapter we shall be primarily concerned with the use of explicit process interventions in 'personal process work'. The term 'personal process work' is used to describe the joint activity between the trainer and trainee in helping the latter to develop an awareness of himself and the ways in which he makes relationships, with particular attention to underlying meanings and feelings. This activity involves the trainer making a number of consecutive explicit process interventions; for example:

Trainer: What are you doing, Jim? (Non-interpretative)
Jim: (Who has been silent and looks very tense) I'm thinking.
Trainer: Tell me what you are thinking. (Directive)
Jim: I'm trying to find the right words to give Peter (another trainee) some feedback.
Trainer: How about taking the risk of giving feedback using the wrong words? (Directive)
Jim: OK . . . Peter, I don't like you.
Trainer: Are those the right words, Jim? (Non-interpretative)
Jim: Yes (smiling). That's what I wanted to say.

In the situation described above, the trainer has asked Jim to describe what he is doing and in responding Jim has discovered that he limits his behaviour (in this case giving feedback) by trying to identify –

through thinking – the right words. On completion of the feedback and Peter's response the trainer will probably check with Jim whether his concern for the 'right words' is a regular feature of his communication process and together they may then explore what he experiences at such time.

Personal process work is likely to cover one or all of the following areas:

1 Exploring feelings (or lack of them)
2 Exploring behaviour moment to moment i.e., words used (or as in the example with Jim, the unspoken words); range of non-verbal behaviour (bodily movements, facial expression, eye contact, changes in breathing patterns etc.).
3 Exploring rules of behaviour e.g. I must not show my feelings
4 Exploring needs/wants/demands of others e.g. I want you to pay attention to me
5 Exploring internal conflicts i.e., between rules and needs (If I don't allow myself to express feelings, how do I get you to pay attention to me?)
6 Exploring external conflicts i.e., problem relationships
7 Exploring perceptions of self and/or others e.g. I am inadequate

Irrespective of the starting point, a piece of personal process work often moves quickly and easily between the above areas.

CHARACTERISTICS OF PERSONAL PROCESS WORK

Although at first sight there appears to be some overlap with counselling personal process work has some important distinguishing characteristics:

1 The 'work' takes place in a training group – and the group is a vital form of support for the individual.
2 The group offers this support by:
    (a) Being there – and, therefore, implicitly (sometimes explicitly) giving permission to the individual to work on the issue
    (b) Acting as resource/audience for the individual's experiments with behaviour
    (c) Giving feedback to the individual and trainer on completion of the work, e.g. I appreciate your courage in exploring this issue.
    (d) Sharing feelings that they experienced during the piece of work, e.g. When you were expressing your

resentment of your boss, I was aware of feeling angry and excited.

(e)   Sharing any experiences that are similar to the issues worked on by the individual, e.g. I now realise that when I am dealing with someone who is being aggressive with me I also try to suppress my anger and try to be reasonable.

This support is vital to the individual because in exploring new patterns of behaviour for himself, or in making explicit old internal conflicts and previously unexpressed feelings, the danger is that he can feel isolated, strange and peculiar. To hear from others that they, too, have had similar experiences, feelings and dilemmas enables the individual – through the group's acceptance of him – to accept who he is.

3   The work is not necessarily concerned with problem resolution or future action. As a result of the exploration the individual may make new decisions or change his behaviour but this is not a primary aim. The 'objective' of the work is for the individual to discover more about who he is and what he wants from others. This development of awareness is the cornerstone of behaviour change in the feeling approach. When the individual, for instance, discovers how he stops himself giving positive appreciations to others he is in a position to make choices about his behaviour;

Does he want to continue with his old behaviour?

Does he want to offer positive appreciations? If so, in what ways can he do this?

If he wishes he can experiment with different ways of giving appreciations;

non-verbal appreciation (smiling, handshaking, offering eye contact, arm round the shoulder etc), verbal appreciation (openly agreeing with others' statements, appreciating what others do – I like the way you asked that question, appreciating qualities in others – I like you etc.)

Having experimented with some of the choices in the group, he is then in a position to make decisions about how he wants to behave back at work.

Having said openly to someone in the group 'I like you', he discovers that not only does he feel good about himself (despite his worst expectations) but that the other person responded favourably to the appreciation and that as a consequence the relationship is closer and more effective. This experience provides the platform for the individual to then use this behaviour back at work.

(This model – awareness, choices, experimentation and decisions – has already been mentioned in Chapter 1, on p. 14.) Personal process work may begin with a person at any one of the four stages (awareness, choices, experiments, decisions) but it does not have to complete all four to be an effective experience.

4   'Here and now' feelings and behaviour are the currency. Where the person is exploring a previous experience or communication with another individual (even if it occurred two minutes ago) he is encouraged to pay attention to what he is feeling and doing now. By paying attention to current experiences he has access to the whole range of information (feelings, physical sensations etc.) that he needs in order to explore the issue. To work in the 'there and then' (relying on memory) limits the information and makes it more difficult for him to focus on what he wants to do now.

Two other characteristics of personal process work which are common to counselling are:

1   It takes time (3 minutes – 2 hours). In terms of our experiences these are offered as outer limits. In less than three minutes the trainer is unlikely to be engaged in personal process work but rather making explicit process interventions or offering feedback. To work with an individual beyond two hours is likely to be unproductive (simply in terms of stamina) and probably indicates that the trainer and trainee are locked into some self-defeating behaviour, i.e. the trainer may be taking too much responsibility for the work or is working – through the individual – on his own issues; the trainee is 'performing' for the trainer and/or himself: the trainee is resisting learning and the trainer is pushing against the resistance.

2   It is completed when the trainee and/or the trainer agrees to stop (with luck this is a joint decision). The trainer may choose to stop working with an individual for a number of reasons:

   (a)   Time constraints – the issue raised by the individual may (in the trainer's judgement) require more time than is immediately available. To begin work on an emotionally-charged issue ten minutes before a programme break is not a good choice for the individual, trainer or group.

   (b)   Lack of self-support – when the trainee does not have the necessary self-support systems (usually he is more scared than excited or interested in doing the work). In this case the trainer is more likely to work at helping the individual develop his level of support.

(c) Lack of external support – the group has not yet developed sufficient trust and openness to provide the individual with the support and acceptance he needs to explore the issue.

(d) Limits of expertise – the trainer feels that the issue raised by the individual (e.g. sexuality, violence, suicide etc.) is beyond his level of expertise. Here it is important for the trainer to be honest about his discomfort and to suggest to the individual where he might find expert help.

(e) Outside the contract – when the issue raised is outside the objectives of the programme. For example, where the trainee wants to explore his relationship with his spouse on a programme that is solely concerned with work-related areas. In this case the trainer may refer the individual to more appropriate training centres or external expertise or may offer one-to-one counselling outside the programme.

(f) The trainer is tired, feels unclear about his own boundaries or feels in need of support from one of his colleagues. At such times he is likely to be open with the trainee about his decision and to suggest that he raises the issue at a more appropriate time.

PERSONAL PROCESS WORK AND THE THINKING, DOING AND FEELING APPROACHES

Clearly, for the trainer to engage in personal process work in a thinking approach programme would be an act of irresponsibility. On thinking/doing programmes, however, the trainer may decide to work with an individual who seems to be experiencing a 'crisis' (e.g. heavily punishing himself with negative feedback). But even here such a decision would be exceptional – the trainer is more likely to make implicit process interventions in the training room (e.g. diverting attention, introducing theory etc.) and then talk to the individual outside the session. On doing/feeling programmes, where the trainer is working with skills and personal process (e.g. counselling skills, training of interpersonal skills trainers, assertion and influencing programmes) then some degree of personal process work is likely to take place. One of the key issues on such programmes is timing. On a

5-day programme the trainer is unlikely to make excursions into this area until the third and fourth day, by which time the necessary levels of trust, support and openness should have been established.

On feeling-based programmes the major learning activity is likely to be some form of personal process work. The reason for this is that a number of current approaches in this area (e.g. sensitivity groups, Encounter, Gestalt, Transactional Analysis, Psychodrama, Bioenergetics) share some common assumptions about the nature of man and the way he learns and develops. (These values and the approaches are drawn from humanistic psychology[1]) The assumptions are:

1   Man is a whole who is (rather than has) a body, emotions, thoughts, sensations and perceptions, all of which interrelate. To focus on just one or two of these areas (e.g. as often happens with the thinking and doing approaches) is to exclude equally valid sources of information and in the process to encourage the fragmentation of the individual. Much of our traditional education and training is solely concerned with developing intellectual skills and abilities and is little concerned with the other areas.

2   Feelings are an important dimension in relationships and generally should be expressed rather than repressed. The emphasis on feelings in these programmes is deliberate and is intended to help an individual to begin the process of accepting and integrating what he may experience as discrete parts of himself. By becoming aware of feelings and physical sensations as they occur he is more able to understand who he is and what he wants from other people. This emphasis, of course, contrasts severely with his previous educational and learning experiences. His immediate response to the programme – anger, excitement, hostility, cynicism, fear – is the usual starting point for personal process work.

3   There are no right answers. Each person, who is by definition unique, must discover his own needs and the needs of others and how to satisfy those needs.

4   Learning how to satisfy those needs can only take place when the individual begins to experiment with his behaviour. (see p. 39)

5   Man is neither intrinsically good nor bad. He is not flawed in some way, e.g. as in the Christian concept of original sin; neither is he engaged in some continuing conflict with a dark side of his personality, e.g. Freud's concept of the Id. He does

have the potential for change and growth – of assimilating rejected parts of himself, resolving internal conflicts between rules and wants, and of taking responsibility for himself and his needs.

With these assumptions as a base each trainer develops an approach to leading others in personal process work that is right for him. The approach that he develops will be shaped by:

1 Theoretical models (e.g. Appendices A and B on the use of TA and Gestalt in personal process work)
2 His own experiences of being on the receiving end of personal process work. It is our belief (see Chapter 6) that the trainer needs to have extensive, and continuing, experience of personal development in order to be effective with trainees on feeling-based programmes.

There is no 'right' approach or method – in fact, effective work with an individual is likely to be determined by the trainer's ability to improvise in response to the needs of each individual. The intervention that worked with one person could well be totally ineffective with another. In this sense, the trainee and not the trainer is the real source for all effective interventions – he knows what works for him.

GENERAL ISSUES IN PERSONAL PROCESS WORK

Irrespective of the underlying model and style used by the trainer there are some general issues about personal process work which will influence his choice of interventions. These issues are:

1 Individual versus group – how and to what end does the trainer make interventions at the level of group rather than individual behaviour?
2 The trainer's relationship with the group – what are the dynamics of this relationship? What does the trainer need to be aware of?
3 Co-training – if there is more than one trainer in the group, how does this affect the relationship with the group?
4 Integrating the learning – in feeling-based programmes what responsibility does the trainer have for ensuring that individuals have integrated their learning?

Individual versus group

Obviously, the model of explicit process interventions mentioned in Chapter 2 can also be used with a group as well as with an individual, for example;

What are you doing in this silence? (Non-directive)
The quality of feedback in this group is poor (Evaluative)
I feel bored with you. (Sharing feelings).

On those feeling-based programmes where the focus of attention is on the individual, the number of explicit process interventions aimed at the group will obviously be small. The trainer is more likely to use implicit process interventions aimed at the group (e.g. pre-course information, setting groundrules for the programme, modelling etc). There are occasions, however, when the trainer will choose to make explicit process interventions aimed at the group instead of engaging individuals in personal process work.

1   At the start of a programme – in the early stages of a training group much of their interest and concern will be with the group itself – who are the members? How will they work together? Is it possible for individuals to feel safe and satisfied? Therefore, the aim of the trainer for the first twenty-four hours of the programme will be to encourage them to raise and explore these issues. One way he will encourage this activity will be to make few interventions, allowing the group to sort these issues out for themselves. His interventions with individuals will be largely concerned with the mechanics of communication – how individuals avoid contact with others, how they break contact, how they give and receive feedback etc. These situations will also provide him with the opportunity to make explicit process interventions to the group.

Pay attention to the way you offer feedback. (Directive)
Pay attention to what you are doing as you speak to each other. (Directive)
Be direct with each other. (Directive)

Until the mechanics are established and individuals feel safe and ready to trust the group and the trainer then the possibility of effective personal process work is minimal.

2   When the group is behaving dysfunctionally, i.e. a significant number of individuals in the group are 'stuck' in a pattern of behaviour e.g. passive, dependent on the trainer, fighting the trainer and/or others in the group, avoiding learning etc. On these occasions the trainer may choose to

confront the group process rather than attempt to work with individuals. Typical interventions in such circumstances may be:

What do you want to do? (Non-directive)
What do you want from me? (Non-directive)
I don't like the way you are behaving. (Evaluative)
How are you stopping yourself learning? (Non-directive)
I feel angry and frustrated with you. (Sharing feelings)

It is important that when the trainer chooses to use the higher risk interventions with the group (e.g. 'I don't like the way that you are behaving') that he is prepared to maintain contact and follow through with his interventions, e.g. 'I am interested in our discovering a way of working together' (Non-directive). Paradoxically, another choice the trainer has for removing the deadlock with a group is to engage individuals in personal process work. By working through issues with one person, e.g. 'How are you making yourself passive?' (Non-directive), the other people in the group make that discovery for themselves and are able to move out of their impasse. When choosing to work this way the trainer needs to be highly directive with the group, e.g. cutting across interruptions, ignoring significant non-verbal behaviour of other individuals, telling the group when and how to give feedback to the person he is working with.

3   Giving recognition and appreciation – as well as giving appreciation and recognition to individuals the trainer may choose to make similar interventions at the group level. This is particularly important when the group has moved through an impasse, e.g.;

I like the way you are offering support to each other. (Positive)
I enjoy working with you. (Positive)

Irrespective of their own level of personal satisfaction, the group members are also likely to be concerned about the group and the way it performs.

The role of the trainer

When using feeling-based programmes the trainer's relationship with the group is an important dimension of learning. For each trainee the decision to trust the trainer is an important and explicit issue. This decision can be a complex one for many individuals because they bring to that relationship a wealth of experience from previous encounters with authority figures, i.e. parents, teachers, bosses.

Their experiences and feelings – and this process is encouraged by the trainer offering minimal structure and guidance at the start of the programme – are then projected on to the trainer. Therefore, different individuals are likely to see the same trainer as either the expert or Mr Wonderful, or as being dishonest, cruel, or uncaring, and will actively look for behaviour that confirms their projection and in the process discard experiences that contradict their image. For many trainees this process is short-lived, they can quickly 'own' their projections, i.e. recognise the process and identify who the trainer really is. For some, however, the projection is based on highly-emotive 'unfinished business' – a term that describes unresolved conflict, unexpressed feelings, unsatisfied needs – and they are 'unable' to move away from it until they have identified the unfinished business through personal process work.

For example, the individual who persists in seeing the trainer as sadistic – in spite of his own experiences, and the experiences and perceptions of other trainees with that trainer – will need to become aware of his own unexpressed feelings towards a sadistic parent or teacher in his past before he is able to make the decision to trust the trainer. For the trainer on the receiving end of such a projection, working with the individual can be an uncomfortable and difficult experience. The reason for this is that the projection may well be founded on some reality of observable behaviour, however small, and the trainer has difficulty in accepting that particular part of himself. (This lack of acceptance is an indicator that he too has unfinished business in this area.) On such occasions the trainer needs to pay particular attention to keeping his own unfinished business clear of the work he does with the individual. If the trainer does lose sight of the boundary between himself and the individual he is likely to be ineffective. For example:

Trainee: You are sadistic!
Trainer: No, I am not!

(In refusing to accept the feedback the trainer is supporting the trainee's process of projection as well as breaking contact with him.)

The danger of the trainer confusing himself with others in this way is a recurring issue on a feeling – based programme. To avoid this danger does not mean that to be effective the trainer needs to have total awareness of himself and to have resolved all his own unfinished business (even if this were possible). What is important, however, is that the trainer is aware of how he can be 'hooked' by a trainee into using compulsive patterns of behaviour. For example: the trainer who does not give himself permission to be confused – and at the first hint of confusion seeks order and clarity – is unable to offer that permission to the trainee. So a typical intervention he might make will be as follows:

Trainee   I am confused . . . and I don't like being confused.

Trainer: Alright. What do you want? (Non-directive)

There is a strong possibility here that both end up feeling confused. A more effective intervention in this situation would be:

Trainer: What is it like being confused? (Non-directive)

In terms of helping the trainee to make the decision to trust him, the trainer needs to be able to keep himself clear and detached from the trainee. The other behaviours that the trainer must exhibit to build trust are:

1   His willingness both to confront the behaviour of the trainee and to offer support, e.g.;

> I don't like the way you choose to fight me and I'm interested in finding some other way for us to relate to each other. (Evaluative)

2   His willingness to share feelings both 'good' and 'bad'

3   His willingness to accept the individual and his feedback even when he expressed disagreement with it, e.g.;

> I accept that you regard me as being tough on you – although I feel interested in you rather than tough. How can I be 'soft' with you? (Non-directive)

4   His willingness to offer permissions to the trainee

> It's alright to feel scared. (Cathartic)
>
> You don't have to do a perfect job. (Directive)

To find the right balance between, on the one hand, offering support and, on the other, confrontation can be difficult for both the trainer and trainee. For, in order to be effective in leading others in personal process work, the trainer needs to be skilled in being able to frustrate the individual when he behaves in compulsive ways. For example, the trainee whose primary concern is to be nice to everyone he meets – and in behaving this way feels dissatisfied because, inevitably, those around him do not feel that they are special to him – is likely to be confronted by the trainer with the paradoxical intervention, 'To be nice to me I want you to tell me what you don't like about me'. (Directive) The objective of the intervention is to frustrate him: by denying him the expected response, he is confronted with what he is doing. The consequence for him of such intervention is uncertainty and confusion (i.e. his world no longer makes any sense). The choice he has at this stage is to behave in a new way – in the example above give negative feedback to the trainer – and thereby resolve his confusion. To frustrate the individual in this way is the best form of support that the trainer can offer. It is only at the conclusion of the work that the trainee is likely to understand that the frustration was a form of support.

There is one aspect of the trainer's role of 'projection screen' which can present particular difficulties for him and that is the issue of sexuality. Within any group learning about relationships the way individuals recognise, manage and use their sexual needs is an important and particularly emotive issue. With a group of men and women this issue often emerges from the behaviour of one or two individuals e.g. the person who uses flirting as the only way of gaining attention from others; the behaviour of two individuals in the group who are strongly attracted to each other etc. In spite of the 'sexual revolution' of the 1960s, it is our experience that for the majority of people dealing with sexuality is still a very uncomfortable and difficult experience. One consequence of this discomfort is that their unexpressed feelings and fears can be projected on to the trainer – he may be seen by some individuals as sexually skilled, homosexual, manipulative etc. When these perceptions are expressed then the trainer can work with the individual on them. Often, however, because of the nature of the subject, individuals are unwilling to be explicit with the trainer (though they may well share these views with other trainees), and are more likely to raise their concern through jokes or joking questions. For example:

Trainee: Do you often put your arm around other men? (big smile)
Trainer: What is the statement behind your question? (Interpretative)
Trainee: (looking uncomfortable) Well, it's a bit queer.
Trainer: What is the 'it'? (Non-directive)
Trainee: Well, you.
Trainer: So, you imagine I am homosexual? (Descriptive)
Trainee: Well . . .
Trainer: How is this important to you? (Non-directive)

The trainer might then explore with the course member his feelings about homosexuality in others and himself. What is important for the trainer is to be sensitive to the individual's discomfort and the ways in which he will manifest his concern. At the same time he needs to be clear about his own feelings about his sexuality and the ways in which he uses his sexual energy in his relationships with both men and women. If he is unclear then the great danger is that he will collude with individuals in their discomfort, e.g. *Trainer*: 'I am certainly not a homosexual! ' and confirm their original perception (i.e. the trainee is convinced that the trainer is lying). By being prepared to accept and work with the projection the trainer is implicitly giving the same permission to the trainee to accept that part of himself.

Co-training

After looking at the nature of the relationship between the trainer and the group it might seem at first sight that when two or more trainers are involved with a programme then the problems identified above are simply increased by a factor of two or three (depending on the number of trainers). In fact, co-training provides some very useful safety nets against these problems.

For instance, the role of the trainer as projection screen becomes clearer when more than one trainer is involved. One reason for this is that the individual is more sensitive to his projections because he is working with two or more trainers (e.g. how does he make one of them more important than the other? or how is it that he feels more comfortable with one than the other?). The continuing contrast between them helps the course member to bring the issue into clearer focus. Quite often, the contrast of his responses can be enormous – one trainer is seen as 'good-Daddy' and the other as 'bad-Daddy' (see p. 35). By having two or more models to work with the trainee's potential learning about himself is significantly increased.

The second reason for increased clarity is that when the course member is working on his projections with one trainer the other trainer can act as arbitrator and intermediary between them.

Trainee (to Trainer 1): I don't trust you.

Trainer 2: What are your suspicions? (Non-directive)

The advantages in this situation are: one, trainer 2 is less likely to confuse his process with that of the trainee, and, two, by working with trainer 2 in this situation, the trainee is likely to feel more comfortable and less pressurised. The third advantage of co-training is that one trainer can give the other feedback when he sees him 'stuck' with a course member.

Trainee (to Trainer 1): I don't like you.

Trainer 1: (Silence)

Trainer 2 (to Trainer 1): Judging by your silence, you're finding it difficult to cope with his comment (Interpretative)

A further advantage of co-training is that outside sessions, as well as during sessions, the trainers can exchange feedback on their experiences with the group and each other. This feedback is one important way in which the trainer can maintain a clearer awareness of who he is and the effectiveness of his interventions with the group. By working effectively together in this way the trainers are able to offer significantly more to the group than one on his own no matter how capable he is.

In order to achieve these advantages, however, it is crucially important that the trainers have a clear understanding of each other and have the resources to work through problems – and these will inevitably occur – in their relationship. If the trainers carry into programmes unfinished business between them then this significantly reduces the level of their effectiveness with the group. For each of them, at best, will be distracted by their unfinished business and this will significantly affect the level and quality of their awareness of course members, and at worst will mean that they end up competing with each other for the group's attention and approval. To complicate the situation further, course members will quickly identify the problem between the trainers and some will use that knowledge to play off one against the other. Even where this does not occur, knowledge of the unfinished business will seriously damage the credibility of the trainers with the group – they are not practising what they preach.

In addition to sorting out the problems as they go along, an effective training team needs to have a clear understanding of both a common approach to training and also of underlying values. For example, if one trainer restricts himself to work-related issues while the other is ready to work with all the interpersonal issues presented by course members (including those concerning his family and social life) then the group is likely to feel confused. Similarly, if one trainer works with the value that it may be a good choice to leave a course member feeling confused or unhappy for a period of time while his colleague believes that such a decision is inappropriate, the likely outcome is that not only do they get in each other's way but they also cut across the potential learning of the trainee, (i.e. they are more concerned with their own needs and values than they are with the trainee's).

The need for a shared understanding of approach and a common set of values does not mean that they have to aim for a common identity. Part of the understanding necessary means both an awareness and acceptance of differences in style and personality. Within a training team the conscious development of individual styles and approaches to personal process work enriches the learning opportunities that can be offered to groups. For example, as a team we draw on a number of approaches in our work – most significantly from TA and Gestalt (see Appendices A and B) – and there are differences in both our ways of working with individuals as well as in our personalities. Because of these differences, we can as a team, be seen as inconsistent. What we feel to be important is to be open with each other and the group on those few occasions where we differ on the choices we exercise with groups and individuals. When there is a difference of opinion between the trainers on how an individual may work on his issue, the options are offered to him for a decision.

Integrating the learning

Although the main aim of feeling-based programmes is to develop awareness of feelings and physical sensations, it is our belief that effective personal learning must also involve both the individual's thinking processes and his values. (In TA terms there is a need to engage Parent, Adult and Child – see Appendix A). To this end an effective programme must provide some models/theory to individuals and must present and provide scope for discussing the often implicit values underlying the approach. (One example of how this can be achieved is presented in the next chapter.)

Other mechanisms for assisting individuals to integrate their learning are:

1 Operating with the expectation that individuals on programmes do not take away more unfinished business than they came with. This expectation needs to be made clear to the group and formal programme time, particularly at the end of the course, should be provided for this purpose.

2 During this programme, course members have time allocated to them in which they are encouraged to reflect on their experiences.

3 When working with an individual on the last day of the programme, the trainer should take greater responsibility with the individual for 'closing down' the issue that he has raised. This closing down will involve moving out of exploring feelings and into the area of behavioural options. For example, if the individual is concerned about his responses to authority figures – instead of exploring his feelings or his unfinished business with historical 'parent figures' – the trainer is likely to invite him to identify a number of options for responding to a specific person at work. Having identified the options – and here the trainer may ask the individual to write these choices down so he has a record of the experience – the individual is then encouraged to identify a particular strategy he would be happy to experiment with. Having done this, the trainer is then likely to invite the person, firstly, to identify the sources of support he can draw on when experimenting and, secondly, to identify a way of rewarding himself for having carried out the experiment. When working with the individual in this way, the trainer is, particularly and deliberately, engaging at the thinking level.

4 Offering post-course support to the group (See Chapter 5).

To ensure that people leave programmes with a clear view, well integrated and ready to meet the outside world is an important ethical and professional responsibility for the trainer. (See Chapter 5). The degree to which any trainer can exercise this responsibility is fundamentally determined by each individual on the programme (i.e. their willingness to raise and work through unfinished business; their capacity and resilience in coping with being stuck with an ineffective pattern of behaviour). Those individuals who have been carrying 'unfinished business' for 20, 30 or 40 years have demonstrated their ability to cope and survive. Their choice to leave the programme unresolved, or with additional unfinished business is – at the end of the day – their choice. All the trainer can do in these circumstances is to offer as many invitations as possible to the individual.

Some individuals who attend feeling-based programmes – in our experience, they are remarkably few in number – can be particularly 'at risk'. Those 'at risk' may be either currently experiencing a serious crisis in their lives (divorce, death in the family etc.) and are, therefore, particularly vulnerable, or they may be people who, for various reasons, lack some basic mechanism for coping with themselves and other people (e.g. the person who vacillates between rigid self-control and destructive, violent behaviour). The trainer's response to handling people at risk will be determined by the individual's self-support system, the level of trust and support in the group and the trainer's level of competence and support systems. The strategic options for dealing with such people are:

1 Agreeing with the individual in or out of session that it is in both their interests that he leaves the programme. Having made the decision the trainer should provide whatever support the person then requires e.g. jointly talking through the issue with the nominating organisation, providing information to the individual on where he can receive specialist support etc.
2 Refusing to engage the individual in any form of personal process work during programme time.
3 Only working with the individual at a thinking level, i.e. behavioural options.
4 Working through the issue with the individual.

By being aware of these options, the trainer can significantly reduce the possibility of an individual leaving the programme in a state of risk. (See also Chapter 5 pp. 107–8 which outlines some of the ethical issues concerning people 'at risk').

The objectives of the trainer on a feeling-based programme is to help people:

1 To take greater responsibility for their own lives.

2 To develop the skills of building adequate support systems (both internal and external).
3 To be sensitive to the needs and feelings of other people.
4 To be willing to accept others.
5 To operate on the assumption that it is possible to increase their level of personal satisfaction with themselves and in their relationships.
6 To understand more fully their impact on others.

The primary vehicle for offering that help is personal process work.

Reference

1 Shaffer John B.P. *Humanistic Psychology*, Prentice-Hall, 1978

4
INTERPERSONAL RELATIONSHIPS IN ORGANISATIONS

INTRODUCTION

This chapter has been written to provide an example of a course based largely on personal process work. The course, titled 'Interpersonal Relationships in Organisations',[1] (IRO for short), lasts for five days, with a maximum of twelve course members, and usually three, occasionally two, trainers.

The aims of this chapter are to give the reader an understanding of the following:

1 The rationale for the course;
2 The important design elements and features;
3 The development of the course;
4 The relationship between the course and the chief ideas presented in the first three chapters.

In addition, the chapter provides an insight firstly into what it feels like to be involved in the course from a trainer's viewpoint and, to some extent, from a participant's; and secondly, the outcomes for participants.

The section describing the feelings experienced by one of the authors working on the course is to help the reader 'get inside the experience' and has therefore been written partly in the first person. While this may contrast sharply with the rest of the book, it is hoped that the different type face used to signal the switches in style will aid rather than interfere with the reader's understanding.

AIMS AND RATIONALE OF IRO

Aims

The overall aims of the course are for participants to:

1 Gain a greater awareness of themselves and their impact on others;
2 Learn about their reactions to others;
3 Increase the range of options which they have in managing relationships;
4 Use their experiences in the training group as a basis for learning about and dealing with work related problems, e.g. authority and influence, membership and leadership issues, power, conflict and cooperation.

These aims are stated in the pre-course notes sent to each intending participant beforehand. These aims also provide a framework within which individuals can define specific personal goals for themselves both before and during the course. The importance of specific personal goals is highlighted in the rationale for the course (also part of the pre-course notes).

Rationale

The course gives the manager, supervisor and specialist an opportunity to review and reflect on their values and their approaches to handling relationships, all with particular emphasis on the organisational context. With up to eleven others, participants are able to re-appraise their attitude to themselves and to work relationships, and are able to explore specific points of concern. These may be points which the participant has come to realise for himself, or they may be the result of comments from others (e.g. boss, colleagues or subordinates).

Within this setting the course members can learn a great deal if they are willing to listen to, and work with, the wide range of feedback which will be available from their course colleagues. The tutors encourage this process by largely avoiding the 'traditional' teaching role of lecturing, setting up role-plays, leading discussions and initiating various task activities. Rather their main aim and responsibility is to encourage the group to focus on the 'here and now' and to pay attention to feelings, relationships and non-verbal behaviour as they occur in the training group.

The reasoning behind this approach is that people can learn a great deal about themselves not only by giving and receiving feedback (i.e.

being honest with each other about what they like and dislike about each other) but by identifying and expressing feelings (e.g. pleasure, anger, sadness, excitement, concern, inadequacy) and also simply by considering carefully what they see going on around them (e.g. 'How come those two seem to be on the same wavelength so quickly?'; 'Why do I feel 'one-down' in my relationship with that person?'; 'What is my responsibility, if any, towards those two people over there who are having an argument?').

As a consequence of this the participants are encouraged to relate their organisational experience to the immediate context of the training group. For example, a course participant may feel that he lacks self-confidence at work. The course provides a great deal of scope for looking at this through exploring the levels of self-confidence of the person in his relationship with the other members of the training group. The trainer's experience and belief is that, more often than not, the key patterns which people develop in their relationships (e.g. collaborative, fighting, warm, distant, caring etc.) are maintained whether at work or on a training course. It is this pattern which, in the context of the course, provides a link between the 'here and now' and the work environment.

Another example is the individual who believes himself to be, or has been told that he is, too aggressive. If he wants to consider this on the course then the tutors will *not* want him to talk in detail about his work relationships, rather they will point out ways in which he can use the training group for learning, e.g;

Do you feel aggressive towards anyone here?
Do you want to get some feedback from others in the group in terms of whether they see you as at all aggressive?
If you were to be aggressive towards anybody here, who would it be?

Whatever the responsibilities of the trainers, (see Chapter 5) the participants have responsibilities too which they have to assume if the course is to be successful for them. These include not only defining and developing specific learning goals, but also

1 Being willing to express concerns, interests and feelings;
2 Being 'reasonably' open; not totally open about everything but at least stating what they see or believe is happening in the group and what they feel about it;
3 Being willing to offer feedback if they have it;
4 Being willing to listen and consider feedback whilst reserving the right not to accept it;
5 Experimenting with different ways of handling relationships.

Underlying these responsibilities is a need for participants to approach the course on a basis of mutual exploration rather than trying to prove particular points.

PARTICIPANTS

As indicated in the previous section, participants attend the course by virtue of their experiences and needs in their current roles. The background to their involvement is that they are in positions where skills with relationships are seen to be important to their effectiveness. This might be in terms of handling subordinates, colleagues, authority figures or clients. Consequently, the composition of any group may be variable, including young and old; male and female; with considerable or little work experience; very junior or very senior in terms of their organisation's hierarchy.

A general requirement for the course is that each of the twelve participants should come from different organisations. Occasionally there are exceptions when the organisations are sufficiently large for two people from the same organisation not to know each other, and where it is unlikely that they will be having contact at work in the foreseeable future.

In general terms, individuals come to pursue the opportunities presented in the aims and rationale described in the previous section. More specifically, people attend for two particular reasons:

1 For developmental purposes, supported by an already effective range of personal relationships skills;
2 For 'remedial' purposes, because of significant difficulties in their organisational relationships, e.g. inappropriate use of aggression or passivity.

For many individuals there are elements of both. In some cases individuals come to the course on their own initiative and others because it was initially their boss's idea. In both cases, feedback about their behaviour from others in the organisation is likely to be a significant factor in stimulating their interest.

Whatever the reasons and circumstances for their nomination, participants go through a two-part 'screening' activity involving:

1 Receipt of the pre-course notes, which have been referred to earlier. These will have been examined and discussed by all the interested parties (prospective participant, his boss, and any personnel and training specialists involved), particularly in relation to the participant's responsibilities.

2   A pre-course telephone discussion between the nominee and one of the training team, to check the nominee's suitability and willingness to attend, and his understanding of the nature of the programme. The important point of willingness is explored in detail since a conscripted course member is unlikely to learn much, he may impede the learning of others, and make the work of the trainers more difficult.

The trainer's responsibilities and actions in this pre-course screening step are discussed more fully in Chapter 5.

DESIGN ELEMENTS AND FEATURES

The course is relatively low in formal structure and is strongly influenced by two important models of personal and interpersonal behaviour, namely Transactional Analysis and Gestalt (see Appendices A & B). However, elements from other approaches may also be introduced on occasions, e.g. Co-counselling, Psychodrama, Sociodrama, Bioenergetics and Encounter groups. In addition, the T-group approach has also been an influence.

The elements of formal structure are shown in the sample programme, Table 4.1, and include introductory activities, small group counselling sessions, personal diary (stock-taking) sessions, a theory session, and closing activities. However the major element in the design is the unstructured group work referred to as 'large group sessions'.

Large group sessions

These are the main 'theatre' for the learning activities, involving all the participants plus one or two trainers. The large group provides a basis for interactions, feedback and personal experiments to occur. The most important work of the trainers takes place in the large group, in a variety of forms, including implicit and explicit process interventions, the management of feedback and personal process work. Illustrations of the latter are included (see pp. 72–82).

Two important considerations with respect to the large group are those of responsibility and energy. In terms of responsibility, the initiative for starting the work of the group lies with the participants; one or more of them starts the interaction and the trainer or trainers follow. A typical intervention by a trainer at the beginning of a large group session is 'The aim of this session is to continue the large group work'. Towards the end of the week, the trainers are likely to forgo

Table 4.1

Sample programme for the IRO course

	Monday	Tuesday	Wednesday	Thursday	Friday
			Personal journal to 9.30 am		
9.15 am		Large group Neil Clark/ Keri Phillips	Large group Dave Barker	Small group counselling Keri Phillips	Closing activities Neil Clark
11.00 am	1.50 Start	Large group Neil Clark/ Keri Phillips	Large group Neil Clark/ Dave Barker	Large group Dave Barker/ Keri Phillips	Closing activities Neil Clark/ Keri Phillips Dave Barker
2.15 pm	On Monday Introductory activities Keri Phillips/ Neil Clark Dave Barker	Large group Keri Phillips	Small group Neil Clark	Large group Neil Clark/ Dave Barker	2.25 pm Finish on Friday
4.00 pm	Introductory activities Keri Phillips/ Neil Clark/ Dave Barker	Large group Keri Phillips/ Dave Barker	Large group Keri Phillips/ Neil Clark	Large group Dave Barker/ Neil Clark	
7.30 pm	Large group Neil Clark	Small group Dave Barker	Large group Keri Phillips	Large group Dave Barker	
9.00 pm					

(Small group may not take place at times stated)

even this minimal intervention. However, the large group sessions, with their 'here and now' focus are often experienced by participants as awkward, unreal, difficult and tense, particularly at the beginning of the week. Consequently, the first large group session after the introductory activities is opened by the trainer offering guidelines for how the group can start and conduct its work. These guidelines are described in Table 4.2. After the presentation of guidelines there is usually an uncomfortable silence before anyone starts.

Table 4.2
Guidelines for the large group session

Exchange first impressions of one another as these can be very important in developing relationships

Start giving and receiving feedback

Look at your relationships, establish them, build on them

Say (more about) what you want to get from the course

Start experimenting with your behaviour

Express any feelings you have; they don't necessarily have to be big, dramatic, or focused

Simply follow your curiosity

As far as energy is concerned there can be whole sessions that are, at least apparently, low in activity, despite the amount of responsibility and initiative group members may have taken at earlier stages in the course. These 'troughs' may be positive in the sense of people taking time to reflect and assimilate after periods of sometimes intense personal process work. They may also be negative, because of a loss of direction and stimulation or an avoidance of important issues. When the group is avoiding issues it may be important for the trainer to be directive by introducing a structured activity as a way of raising the energy (see Appendix C). This, however, runs the risk of creating or recreating too much dependency, so the decision to introduce such an activity is a very finely judged one; it is certainly important for the trainer to make it clear that this step does not mean a serious change in the style of the course, and that a return to the large group process will develop from the review of the activity.

Another choice for handling low energy situations is to invite the group or an individual to take responsibility for initiating such an activity, e.g;

How would you like to spend your time now? (To the group)
Have you an activity in mind that would meet your needs? (To an individual)

A third option, amongst others, is to 'sit things out' until one or more of the participants get sufficiently frustrated and dissatisfied that they spontaneously take the initiative to make something happen.

Introductory activities

These comprise three elements, administrative details, an opening exercise for people literally to introduce themselves to each other, and a statement by one of the trainers describing the nature of the week, including some very important ground rules. A typical opening exercise is shown in Table 4.3.

Table 4.3
Paired introductions

Find a partner and discuss with him the following points for ten minutes each (you may find it useful to take notes).

1   Three positive qualities or skills you have that help you in your relationships with others (apart from technical or professional skills).

2   Up to three qualities you have which you believe get in the way of your relationships with others

3   In what way might you sabotage yourself this week in terms of not gaining what you could from the course (typical examples are – not listening, being consistently 'one-down' or 'one-up', not saying what you want, denying all feedback you receive, setting too high a standard for yourself and/or others).

After the twenty minute period, be prepared to introduce your partner on the basis of these points to the rest of the group.

In this exercise, the participants are deliberately steered away from reference to professional and organisation roles and are asked to focus on how they manage relationships. The paired introduction immediately provides an opportunity for the trainers to make explicit process interventions, e.g;

He told you he is a good listener; is that how he came across to you? You said to your partner that you don't suffer fools gladly; what does that mean for you?

The statements made concerning the nature of the week are shown in Table 4.4.

Table 4.4
The nature of the week

The events of the week are confidential to the extent that there is no reporting back by the trainers on individuals to their organisations.

The programme is flexible and scheduled events may not happen at the programmed times.

One fixed point in the course is the opportunity to complete a personal journal from 9.15 to 9.30 am each morning.

The main focus for the learning is what is happening 'here and now' in the group, i.e. moment by moment. What has happened in the 'there and then' (the past) will only be explored to the extent that it relates to the 'here and now'.

Some of the important things that happen to and between people often happen very quickly. Consequently we shall slow things down so that these events are not missed.

We have a fundamental belief that interpersonal skills are based on choices and consequences rather than rights or wrongs.

The responsibility for learning is shared, and we encourage you to use certain ground|rules which we believe help this learning.

Say 'I' rather than 'we', 'one', 'they', 'people'.

Talk directly to the other person, not about him or her.

Make clear statements rather than asking rhetorical or leading questions.

They reflect much of what is said in the pre-course notes. This may seem repetitive, but experience has shown that it is important for course members to be told as clearly as possible the nature of the experience they are entering. Since the nature of the week is discussed after the personal introductions, there is already some limited process experience available for reference and illustration. The ground rules illustrated in Table 4.4 are Gestalt-based and are offered not as absolute rules of conduct, but as modes of behaviour to help increase the potential learning from the course. The emphasis on choices and consequences in interpersonal relationships is firmly rooted in humanistic psychology (see p. 42).

Small group counselling sessions

The small group counselling sessions usually occur two or three times during the week and normally comprise two to six participants. The sessions have a number of aims:

1   An opportunity to continue the learning in a different format from the large group. This change in format can be particularly welcome if there has been some intense personal process work in the large group.
2   To provide a means for stimulating the group if the energy level is low.
3   An opportunity to exchange feedback and support, particularly for more passive and reticent individuals.

The trainers invite the course members to manage the small groups within the guidelines and ground rules of the course, but otherwise only involve themselves in the counselling discussions if invited to do so by the participants themselves.

Personal journal

The personal journal is illustrated in Table 4.5. It is completed privately (and optionally) from 9.15 to 9.30 am each day. Its aims are:

Table 4.5
Personal journal

Make notes under the following headings:

★ Feedback received	★ My main contribution(s) to the group is (are)
★ Feedback wanted	★ What I want to do today is
★ Feelings about self	★ Feelings about others

You may or may not wish to share these notes in the group.

1 To provide a record for participants of key events and issues
   after the programme as a basis for discussions with other parties
   at work; it can also be a valuable reminder of what can be for
   some people, a particularly significant event in their lives.
2 To provide a vehicle for crystallising thoughts, ideas and
   feelings in relation to their own needs and specific learning
   goals for the course.

While it is very much the property of each individual concerned,
course members are free to share the contents of their journal in the
large or small group sessions.

Theory session

At an appropriate time, one of the large group sessions is given over to
a theory presentation and discussion. The exact point at which the
theory is introduced varies between late Tuesday and late Wednes-
day. The decision when to introduce it depends on two key criteria.
Firstly the evident willingness of at least most of the course members
to work with the learning methods and accept their responsibilities for
the effectiveness of the programme. Secondly as a reflection of the
former that a substantial amount of feedback and explicit process
interventions have occurred, possibly including some personal process work. In addition it is always introduced in a session led by one
tutor only; doing the theory with two tutors is not a good use of
resources.

The reasons for introducing theory on this programme are:

1 To provide a model for people to take a fresh look at who they
   are, and their relationships in the group and at work, including
   problem areas and their specific learning goals
2 To acknowledge the fact that whatever the emphasis on feelings
   in the course, humans are also thinking beings.
3 To provide some respite from the intensity of the large group
   process.

The theory used is Transactional Analysis (TA) (See Appendix A).
The reasons for this choice are:

1 It is a good model for linking the thinking, doing and feeling
   parts of ourselves; it is also an integrated model of personality,
   behaviour and communication.
2 It seems to have a high face validity for most people, both in
   terms of 'explaining' experiences on the course and experiences
   at work.
3 It is sufficiently flexible to fit into a limited period of time.
4 It is one of the two major models used by the trainers in their

work on the course, with concepts that can readily be shared with the participants for the remainder of the week.

The theory is presented as a didactic input, often with reference by the trainer to examples of course members' behaviours so that particular concepts can be illustrated, e.g;

'George, when you told Bill off for interrupting you, you appeared to be in your Critical Parent because of the way you were stabbing your finger at him.'

'John, it seems to me you spend a lot of time in a rescuer role. I've seen you move in to help someone else four times so far this week without checking whether they want your help.'

The participants are encouraged to explore the theory for themselves, with cautions not to use it as a panacea. The maximum time set aside for this theory is usually two hours. At the end of this period the trainer steers the group back to the central activity of the programme, namely large group sessions.

Closing activities

The Friday morning of the programme is taken up with four main activities as follows:

Post-course support This is a presentation by the trainer of ways of maintaining personal effectiveness on leaving the course, together with recommended books, useful addresses and ideas for further development. The issue of post-course support is dealt with further in the next chapter (see pp. 110–11).

Applying the learning This is time spent in small groups for the purpose of actively using the week's experience and learning to resolve, or begin to resolve, personal issues or relationship problems outside the course. An example is shown in Table 4.6.

Finishing business This is time devoted to ensuring, as far as possible, that any unfinished business between individuals is raised and resolved in the large group. In addition, this activity provides an opportunity for individuals to resolve any concerns or issues they have about themselves.

Goodbyes This activity involves the trainers and participants consciously expressing goodbyes to one another in the large group. This may be done in direct terms, e.g. 'I'd like to say my goodbyes to you, Jill, and say how much I've appreciated the support you have given me and others in the group. I'd like to say my goodbyes to you, Mike, and encourage you to spend more time taking care of yourself.'

Alternatively, this can be done indirectly, for example by inviting

Table 4.6
Applying the learning

Organise yourself into small groups of no more than four people.

1   Individually consider the following points:

   a) What changes have you experienced in yourself this week?

   b) What different approaches in relationships have you used or
       experienced from others this week?

   c) Particularly, what has been important for you this week? How
       can you transfer this to work and other relationships that are
       important to you?

2   With the help of your colleagues, consider:

   a) The choices you have

   b) The possible consequences for yourself and the others involved

   c) The support you need, both here and now from your colleagues
       and there and then in the context concerned.

The trainers are available for help should you require them.

---

people to offer one another imaginary gifts, e.g. 'I should like to give
an oak tree for your garden because it represents the strength and
solidity you have shown this week'. The rationale for this stress on
saying goodbye is firstly as a contribution to finishing business and
secondly, to draw attention to the process that is facing the group.
Saying goodbye is a lifelong event, and certainly a recurring one in
organisations. Few people give themselves the opportunity to reflect
on this, the feelings involved, and the consequences for them.

   The balance of time spent on the last three activities will vary from
group to group. For example, some groups will have dealt with their
unfinished business effectively on the Thursday afternoon. Certainly
one of the trainers will raise this as an item to deal with then. Those
groups which have been particularly intensive in terms of personal
process work will need to spend more time on saying goodbyes than
on the other activities.

A BRIEF HISTORY OF THE DEVELOPMENT OF THE COURSE

The decision to develop the course was made in 1975, based on the interests of the trainers and some of their client organisations. Certain characteristics were agreed to be important to the nature of the course:

1   An interpersonal skills course with less emphasis on thinking and doing, and more on the feeling end of the continuum (see Chapter 1).

2   A course which did not rely on learning about such formal, role-dependent interpersonal situations as interviews and meetings (already covered in other courses), but rather looked at the behaviour and skills of the whole person albeit within the context of work.

3   A course which would enable the trainers to develop new skills, and did not consist solely of established approaches such as the T-group or Interaction Analysis.

Subsequently two programmes were run in early 1976, using a blend of two approaches. The more important approach was TA, and involved using extensive theory and exercises and also working with individuals to gain their agreement to tight and specific personal contracts for behaviour change.[2] At the time TA was becoming fashionable as a new approach to interpersonal skills training and seemed to hold significant promise. Some members of the training team undertook further development in the subject to ensure the maximum use of its potential.

The other approach used was structured, sensitivity exercises[3] to explore authority and power, leadership and membership and influence processes in groups. Some of the exercises were Encounter-based in their methods, involving for example, limited physical contact.[4] Such high risk interventions were reflected by the seating arrangements used right from the beginning of the course: an open circle of chairs with no desks. This is still used to this day. Despite these elements of high risk, the course as a whole was quite structured in terms of what activities or exercises were going to be used and when. Even with this structure, the two programmes proved to be different (illustrating the unpredictable nature of feeling-based work) in terms of the development of trust, self-disclosure, the achievement of learning goals and sense of satisfaction at the end.

In short, the first course was a success (with euphoria as well as personal learning) and the second a relative failure, some course members professing not to have derived any benefit at all from it.

From this experience some very important points emerged. The trainers learnt that participants need to come to feeling-based courses at least reasonably willingly and they should also have some understanding of the nature of the experience they are about to enter. This led directly to the use of pre-course telephone discussions with participants, and the development of pre-course notes. The trainers also realised that they needed to be very concerned and clear about their own limits of confidence and competence. Any trainer pushing himself beyond his limits of competence is likely to be at best unhelpful, and at worst destructive, to the participants, as well as sabotaging his own level of satisfaction and effectiveness. This learning reinforced the need for continuous professional and self-development (see Chapter 6).

A third course was run in late 1976, with two innovations which are still used and continue to be important parts of the programme. These were firstly, the use of Gestalt-based ground rules and interventions; this happened after the trainers had received some Gestalt training. Secondly, the Personal Journal was introduced (see Table 4.5).

Two courses were run in 1977, with some key discoveries and changes: An experiment with thirteen participants on the course highlighted the problems for each participant in getting sufficient attention and opportunity to learn when there is just one additional participant. From then the course size was limited to a maximum of twelve.

The Tavistock approach[5] was briefly experimented with in 1977 and then rejected. (This approach is highly interpretative, firmly rooted in psychoanalysis, with the central idea of the existence of group level behaviour independent of the individuals.) At the same time, the composition of the training team was changing, with some leaving and new trainers joining the team.

Four courses were run in 1978 against a background of increasing interest from organisations. Important learning and landmarks that year were as follows:

1   It was usually counterproductive to have more than one person from an organisation on each course, unless it was large and decentralised; the risks of suspicion and mistrust were too high.

2   A significant number of in-company trainers were coming on each course. This was understandable, given their influencing role in their organisations. However, they often competed with the course trainers. Sometimes they formed a powerful sub-group in conflict with the non-trainers for part of the week,

thereby raising opportunities for learning about intergroup issues.

3 The behavioural contracts were largely dropped in favour of Gestalt-based invitations, e.g. 'One thing you can do here is explore how you feel superior to other members of this group'.

Here the implicit process message from the trainer is, 'It's your choice'. This contrasts with the statement, 'I would like you to agree with me that from now on you will stop feeling 'one-down' and bad about yourself'. (An example of a behavioural contract.) The implicit process message from the trainer in this instance is, 'You must change'. The reason for this switch in emphasis was the inherently coercive qualities in behavioural contracts. This often seemed to lead to rebellion or compliance, thereby supporting already established and often unproductive patterns of handling relationships. In any case, many people were not clear enough about their needs to formulate and agree contracts with any precision.

Perhaps the most important development that occurred at this time was the decreased reliance on structured activity and Encounter exercises; and the large group emerged as the main vehicle for personal learning. An approach to manning was also developed that overcame the problem of the trainer being exposed to the group for extended periods thereby becoming tired and losing effectiveness. This manning approach is one of 'overlapping' and is shown in Table 4.1. This enables the trainer re-entering the course to have a handover time with a trainer who has been involved for several sessions. It makes it easier to pick up the threads of the content and process of the group as a whole and also of the individual participants. The handover is successful because of the considerable time spent on discussions by the trainers outside the formal programme.

In 1979, seven courses were held, with the number of training staff increased, and the programme structure finally being established much as it is now. Some of the key events and developments included:

1 The emergence of the three-part format for the start of each course as described above, i.e. administrative details, personal introductions and the 'nature of the week'.
2 The equal establishment of Gestalt with TA for process interventions and personal process work. This underlined the need for the trainers not only to continue their own development in these approaches but also to work at integrating them. This proved to be particularly important where two trainers were working together, one with a Gestalt and the other with a TA orientation.
3 Increased time and attention on the relationships within the

staff team, largely in the form of regular process meetings. These provided opportunities to explore interpersonal issues such as mutual support, and trainer competition, as well as professional issues such as the impact on groups of different trainer styles, and appropriate interventions for handling difficult course members.

4 Considerable attention to work in the large group such as: maintaining the balance between the number of trainer interventions on the one hand, and allowing sufficient interaction between participants on the other; making sure individuals were the focus of both support and confrontation whenever possible; and minimising the extent to which people were put under the 'spotlight' and pressured to perform in some way, e.g. 'It's your turn, you haven't been done yet!'

5 A rationale for the course, as described on pages 55–7 (the broad aims have been a more or less consistent theme from the start of the courses) and criteria for choosing when to introduce small group counselling (see p. 63).

By 1980, the number of courses reached ten per year, (in 1983 the number had increased to twelve). Some features of this period were: considerable discussion and clarification of the boundary between training and therapy – this is examined in Chapter 5 – and the establishment of a format for closing activities. In the background there were fears that the rapidly developing recession would lead to a reduction in the number of courses, based on the course being seen as an irrelevant luxury in the face of diminishing resources. However, this has not proved to be the case. What was noticeable was a change in the qualities and problems brought to the course by participants, e.g. less optimism, more depression, frustration and stress. The trainers' response was to help people find more options for taking care of themselves, including several pages of advice at the end of the programme on maintaining personal effectiveness.

Since 1980, the course has continued with further developments in trainer style and interventions, within the basic theme of an established model. This has been accompanied by further staff changes. However, design and structure are very much a matter of modification, not substantial change.

IRO AND PERSONAL PROCESS WORK

The most important feature of the IRO course in training terms, is the use of personal process work, as defined in Chapter 3. Examples of this approach are illustrated later in this section. What follows now is a review of how IRO relates to some of the important concepts discussed in the previous chapters. In terms of the thinking – doing – feeling continuum, it is firmly based at the feeling end, with the following characteristics:

1 Largely trainee-centred
2 Informal
3 Generally, low trainer direction
4 High process emphasis (the process is the content of the course)
5 Emphasis on trainees finding their own answers to solve problems, based on their own assessment of their needs and also on their own assessment of the value of their learning
6 Almost entirely 'here and now'.

In addition, the trainers support and encourage the exploration of feelings as a legitimate dimension affecting the quality and effectiveness of relationships.

There are excursions to other parts of the continuum most notably with the theory session. However, most of the activity is centred on the process dimension in relationships, in terms of awareness, choices, experiments and decisions as described at the end of Chapter 1 (see p. 14) e.g;

> Are you aware of how tensely you are sitting? What other choices do you have in handling aggressive people? Trying offering him some encouragement instead of criticism. On the basis of what you did in the last session, it seems that you have made a decision this week not to reject people so readily.

Such explicit process interventions are vital themes for the week and the starting point for personal process work. These interventions are often in the form of feedback from the trainer to the trainees. Additionally, the trainers encourage participants to offer one another considerable feedback as a way of raising awareness in the small group counselling sessions as well as the large group. The personal journal offers a way of raising awareness through introspection.

In terms of explicit process intervention style, the emphasis is:

1 *Here and now* with little *there and then* (although a certain amount of there and then discussion is accepted in the early stages of a course while participants are adjusting to the learning approach, and towards the end as preparation for the return to work).
2 More *non-directive* than *directive* (though an example of personal process work is likely to include a number of directive interventions).
3 Mainly *non-interpretative*. Where *interpretative* interventions are

made, they are clearly offered as interpretations to the course member.

4   Mainly *descriptive*. Occasional *evaluative* interventions are made, particularly if there is risk of personal harm, e.g. 'I think it is bad for you to continue helping others so much, I believe that you could well end up feeling exhausted'.

5   *Positive* and *negative*, as appropriate. The large majority of participants are likely to be the focus of both support and confrontation from different people at various times in the programme. Given this mixture of support and confrontation, an important role of the trainer is offering interventions that provide permission and protection.

6   *Cathartic* interventions are used mainly at the level of giving individuals permission to experience feelings, e.g. 'It's OK to be angry', though in some cases the trainer will choose not to do so (see pp. 107–8).

7   Mainly *sharing feelings*, though there are occasions when the trainer will either choose to hold back or to moderate his expression of feelings (see p. 101).

The development of trust and support through explicit and implicit process interventions provides an essential atmosphere for personal process work to take place. Examples of this follow. Some are actual transcripts, others are reconstructed after the event based on the trainer's recollections. In all instances some details have been changed in order to preserve confidentiality.

Example 1

Trainer:	I think it's time to start reviewing and considering whether we have any concerns, or feedback we want to give or get. I'd like to start, and one of my concerns is you, Peter, because you look pretty awful to me.
Peter:	(Slumped and depressed) Yes, you're right.
Trainer:	What's that about?
Peter:	Well, several important things have happened and I didn't pick up the clues. For example, Bill was feeling scared a little while ago and I didn't realise. You said earlier on in the week that you thought I was perceptive, but I don't think so. I feel bad about myself for missing some important things.
Trainer:	You seem to be giving yourself a really hard time.
Peter:	Yes I am.
Trainer:	I don't want you to, and I've got a suggestion in terms of a way forward for you. Are you interested?

Peter:	Yes.
Trainer:	(Going over to sit on the floor in front of Peter) I'd like you to imagine that it's next week and that I am one of your subordinates coming in to see you. As your subordinate I'm feeling really bad about having made a mistake and it's your job to counsel me.
Peter:	Yes . . . OK. Except that if I'm going to counsel you then I want to be on the same level and I'll sit on the floor with you.
Trainer:	(In the role of subordinate, slumped and looking depressed) I feel really bad about a mistake I made earlier today and I'm wondering whether I'm up to this job. Can you help me?
Peter:	I don't know. What's it about?
Trainer:	My judgement about somebody was completely wrong and I feel awful about it.
Peter:	Feeling miserable won't help. There's no point in carrying on like this.
Trainer:	I won't . . . (switching out of role) if you promise to take some of your own good advice. How long are you going to feel miserable for?
Peter:	I don't know.
Trainer:	How about feeling really, *really* miserable for the next five minutes so that you can get it all out of your system and enjoy the rest of the day?
Peter:	(Smiling) I don't think I need to feel miserable even for that period of time.
Trainer:	That's right!

Commentary

When somebody is depressed then energy is nearly always a key issue. Most of the trainer's interventions are therefore concerned with raising the trainee's energy. This is happening at two levels: firstly, the role-play itself (this particular application was borrowed from co-counselling[6]) is likely to generate energy, whether it be in terms of carrying it out or indeed resisting the suggestion. Secondly, there is the teasing from the trainer in the sense that both parties are aware of the issues and the mechanics used to explore them. The trainer's interventions with regard to the role play are so obvious and so transparent that there is some fun in the whole activity, and this fun is a key to releasing energy. It is almost a game if 'I know that you know that I know . . . '

Throughout the exchanges the trainer is being directive, for example in terms of initiating with the individual and also through stating some quite strong values (e.g. 'I don't want you to . . . ') The question of style is debatable here (as it nearly always is!), but the trainer's decision was largely based on time and timing. This was the last afternoon of the course with only a few hours left so there was not a lot of time for a more open-ended exploration of Peter's concerns. Also the trainer believed, from his previous knowledge of Peter, that he would not be 'difficult' in terms of avoiding the issue but would be basically clear, open and direct. The trainer hoped and expected therefore that the personal process work could be completed quite quickly. (The idea of presenting strong values so that somebody is given a clear alternative way of looking at the world can be seen in terms of TA and the use of the Parent ego state: see p. 131.)

A final comment is about the trainer's invitation to Peter to feel *really* miserable. This is based on the assumption that people can identify more options if they allow themselves the opportunity to experience the extremes of any particular feeling which may be important to them, e.g. pleasure, despair, excitement, passivity, power, impotence. (This type of intervention is drawn from Gestalt, see p. 155.) As it turned out, the power of the intervention was in its teasing quality.

Example 2

Joan:	I was talking to Simon earlier on in the week, and it's to do with my relationship with men. There are certain men with whom I get into a one-down position and I don't really assert myself.
Trainer 1:	What sort of men?
Joan:	Well actually, men like Simon.
Trainer 1:	What about telling Simon how you feel about him?
Joan:	Well, alright . . . but I'm not sure what that would achieve.
Trainer 1:	I'm assuming that it would help if you could focus on your concerns by dealing with one specific relationship. If you want to do this, you might start by saying to Simon, I feel one-down to you Simon in the following ways . . .
Joan:	Alright . . . I feel one-down to you Simon because you seem to know more than I do . . . No, this isn't right, I don't feel I'm getting anywhere.
Trainer 2:	You're certainly asserting yourself with us. How about thinking of the type of men you get into a one-down

	position with and reflect on their common characteristics and I'll note them down on this flip chart paper.
Joan:	They're older, forceful, clear in their opinions, often take care of me. In many ways they are like my father.
Trainer 1:	Are there any of these qualities which you would like to have?
Joan:	I would certainly like to be forceful.
Trainer 2:	Well what about being forceful now with one of the members of the group.
Joan:	I don't know what you mean.
Trainer 2:	Have a look round the group, taking your time, and consider whether there is anything forceful which you want to say to anybody.
Joan:	I don't know what you mean by forceful.
Trainer 2:	You define the word for yourself in your own way and take it from there.
Joan:	Alright (looks quickly round the room) . . . No there's nothing I want to say.
Trainer 1:	Take your time.
Joan:	(Looks slowly round the room) No there really isn't anything I want to say.
Trainer 1 (to Trainer 2):	She isn't going to make it easy for us, is she?
Trainer 1:	Another suggestion I've got for a way forward is that you draw a picture. Somehow words are getting in the way here.
Joan:	What sort of picture?
Trainer 1:	Well, a picture which represents the problem you have described, or a picture which indicates what you've got from your work so far. (He puts a large sheet of paper and a felt tip pen in front of Joan. Joan picks up the pen and quite quickly draws a circle.)
Joan:	That's the way I feel, going round in circles.
Trainer 2:	I would like you to be the circle and describe yourself as the circle.
Joan:	What do you mean?
Trainer 2:	Start by saying, I am a circle and I am . . .
Joan:	I am a circle and I am small.
Trainer 2:	What does it feel like to be small?
Joan:	Tight and vulnerable.
Trainer 2:	Are you always like this?
Joan:	No. Sometimes I'm big.
Trainer 2:	Well, draw the circle which represents this other part of you. (Joan draws a large circle.)

Joan:	There.
Trainer 2:	And what's that part of you like?
Joan:	Stronger and more confident.
Trainer 1:	Is there any other part of you that you haven't described yet?
Joan:	I don't know.
Trainer 1:	Have a think about it, and when you're ready, draw it. You may have to turn the paper over for space. (Joan turns the sheet over and draws another circle.)
Trainer 1:	What's that?
Joan:	Another circle. I feel as if I'm going in circles again.
Trainer 2:	Notice how your third circle is a medium circle and fits exactly between the two circles you drew on the other side of the paper. (Joan looks confused)
Trainer 1:	You have all these qualities of being a small, medium and large circle and you can choose when, where and how to be these ways. Do you understand?
Joan:	(Looking a little slumped and perplexed)
Trainer 1:	What I see in you now is the small circle . . . vulnerable and one-down. Support yourself with your posture and breathing and get into your large circle. (Joan sits up and breathes deeply.) Do you feel as if you are in your large circle?
Joan:	Yes.
Trainer 1:	Good. Now turn to Simon and ask for some feedback.
Joan:	Simon. I want some feedback from you.
Simon:	I admire you for what you've done.
Trainer 2:	How are you feeling Joan?
Joan:	Good.
Trainer 2:	Were you a big circle or a small circle?
Joan:	Big circle.
Trainer 2:	Well done. You've clearly got a choice about whether you relate to Simon in a one-down way or not. I think you could have a lot of fun for the rest of the week exploring and using your small, medium and large circles to relate to this group. I think there is enough trust for you to take that risk.
Joan:	I think you're right.
Trainer 1:	(Teasing) Is that small, medium or large circle!

Commentary

In this piece of work there are clearly a number of dead ends. A significant factor here was obviously Joan's own process in that she did and did not want to look at the problem she identified. This ambiguity may well have been outside her awareness. A complicating issue was that Joan's issue concerned men and she was faced with two male trainers who, additionally, were probably seen by her as authority figures.

A number of the interventions (e.g. writing a list on the board and the drawing) are attempts by the trainers to help provide sufficient distance between Joan and themselves so that the process can be more clearly seen.

It was also probably important that the trainers held a consistent line, particularly with the comment, 'She isn't going to make life easy for us, is she?' There were therefore no big differences between the trainers which Joan could have exploited either inside or outside her awareness.

The trainers may be seen as doing more than 50 per cent of the work, but this is another instance of limited time, towards the end of the programme where taking a more low key approach is likely to leave too many loose ends and therefore unfinished business. This was also a reason for not picking up the cue about Joan's relationship with her father. To have followed this through would probably have made the work much higher risk, therefore leading to higher resistance and much more time being required. (Anyway, many trainers would regard the exploration of such a relationship as being therapy rather than training.)

It also seemed with Joan that intellectual/emotional conviction was not enough and that she actually needed to experiment behaviourally in relating to Simon without being one-down. The basis for this assessment was largely intuitive, but it did seem to meet Joan's underlying need for something to be 'proven'.

Example 3

At the beginning of this exchange Terry is reluctant to explore his expressed feeling of superiority to others in the group. By working with one of his images – a room – he was able to discover some unfinished business.

Trainer: In what ways do you feel superior now?

Terry: I am aware of stereotyping people . . . keeping myself above them . . . feeling critical of them.

Trainer: Are you prepared to share your criticisms?

Terry: I don't know if I want to.

Trainer: What would happen if you do?

Terry: I would feel superior to them . . . I can't think . . .

Trainer: What would happen if you lost your superiority?

Terry: I am not altogether sure that it is superiority. I'm beginning to withdraw from the group . . . I don't feel superior now . . . (As he says this he slowly edges his chair back towards the door.)

Trainer: Are you aware of physically moving back?

Terry: I'm aware of doing that . . . I feel blank at the moment . . . I want to fade into the room.

Trainer: O.K., I would like you to close your eyes and describe yourself as this room. Start, I am a room . . . .

Terry: (Very fast) I am a room, four walls, roof, carpet, long window, flip chart, nine people.

Trainer: I suggest you take your time and go through your description and see if anything interests you.

Terry: The walls are cream in colour.

Trainer: Say, I am cream coloured . . .

Terry: I am cream coloured . . . I've got nine people sitting on me . . . (with this statement his voice is slow and laboured)

Trainer: Say that again.

Terry: I've got nine people sitting on me.

Trainer: What does it feel like having nine people sitting on you?

Terry: Very heavy . . . I feel heavy . . . I want to fall asleep. There is a fairly tense atmosphere in me . . . I'm aware of eight people looking at me . . . My eyelids are very heavy . . . I want to open my eyes.

Trainer: Where in your body do you feel tense?

Terry: Across my eyes. I want to open my eyes.

Trainer: How are you stopping yourself?

Terry: I can't . . . I'm getting very, very confused.

Trainer: Are you back in your room?

Terry: (No answer)

Trainer: Are you back in your room? (shouted)

Terry: Yes (opens eyes)

Trainer: I would like you to say to different individuals in the room, 'You are sitting on me and making me feel heavy'.

Terry completes the exercise and identifies three people in the room who he uses to make himself feel heavy. He then describes some connection – their eyes – between these three people and his father with whom he continues to have a difficult relationship.

Commentary

In the example Terry begins with a concern about his feeling of superiority and then quickly begins to experience feelings of inferiority. This shift on his part, which often takes place during the course of personal process work, is a clear illustration of personal polarities i.e. whenever an individual recognises one aspect of himself (e.g. superiority) then the antithesis (e.g. inferiority) is also evident. Only by accepting both these parts of himself will Terry be able to work through his current impasse. This concept of personal polarities is a central feature of the Gestalt approach.

Another important feature in this example of personal process work is how Terry is using his energy from moment to moment. From the earliest exchanges Terry starts turning his energy in upon himself – resisting invitations, becoming blank, silent and then confused. This repressed energy is experienced by Terry as a physical phenomenon e.g. feeling tense and heavy across the eyes. Having encouraged Terry to become aware of this process, the trainer invites him to turn his energy outward i.e. to make contact with other course members, because the clarity that he (i.e. Terry) is seeking can only emerge from making contact with them. In the process of making contact with them he is able to discover the cause of his feelings i.e. the relationship with his father.

This example also illustrates how the use of imagery can provide a quick and powerful vehicle for moving out of an impasse because the individual bypasses many of the blocks and resistances which he may use in other learning situations. (A common block that individuals use is to demand of themselves complete understanding of their behaviour, the reasons for it, and other options, when they are actually in the process of discovery.)

Example 4

In this excerpt Steve has identified an issue which is creating problems in his relationships with senior managers at work.

Steve:	I want to work on the issue of how I make myself tense when dealing with people I respect or fear.
Trainer:	Are you feeling tense now?
Steve:	Yes
Trainer:	Where do you experience the tension?
Steve:	Here (pointing to his abdomen)
Trainer:	I want you to describe yourself as the feeling of tension.
Steve:	I am a spring inside Steve . . . keeping him down.

Trainer:	Say that again.
Steve:	I am keeping him down (slow, solemn voice)
Trainer:	How long have you been inside Steve?
Steve:	(Slowly begins to smile, obviously pleased with his discovery.) Since he was 12.
Trainer:	What happened when you were 12 Steve?
Steve:	I started fighting back against my elder brother who used to bully me.
Trainer:	Do you want to finish up with your brother now?
Steve:	Yes

Steve is invited to do some two-chair work: from one chair Steve talks to his brother, he then switches chairs and continues to dialogue as his brother. The subsequent dialogue clarifies how Steve now avoids conflicts with others because of his fear – learnt from his relationship with his brother – that he will be physically punished for asserting himself.

Commentary

This example illustrates the continuing dilemma facing trainers involved in personal process work, and that is where does he draw the line between training and therapy? (See Chapter 5.) The decision point for the trainer in this case occurs when Steve identifies the unfinished business with his brother. At this point the trainer could make interventions with Steve which keep the work clearly in the arena of training e.g. 'What does that mean for you in your choices for handling authority figures now?' (A non-directive intervention which has the clear intention of switching Steve from his feelings into thinking about solutions). 'Your boss is not your brother.' (A directive intervention which attempts to achieve a similar switch.)

The trainer's decision to invite Steve to go into what many would clearly view as a process of therapy depends on a number of factors. In this case the important factors were:

1 Steve's willingness
2 His level of self-support (in fact was he at this stage more excited than anxious?)
3 The level of group support (the group's willingness to offer him support in the process of discovery).
4 The time available (in this case at the start of a two-hour session).
5 When this occurred on the programme (in this case it was the third day of a five-day programme).
6 The trainer's judgement about the appropriateness of non-

cathartic interventions (as in the examples above) for Steve. Would the unfinished business of his relationship with his brother be so intrusive that decisions to change his behaviour with authority figures be little more than a vague aspiration? (On this occasion the trainer believed that this was a distinct possibility.)

Although this decision making process is made by the trainer the validity of his judgement can only be assessed by the most important person involved in the work – in this case it is Steve.

Example 5

The following shows Mike beginning to explore his relationship with one of the trainers. Until this exchange Mike had avoided making contact and had been content to stay with his projections.

Mike: (To Trainer 1) I feel suspicious of you . . . I don't trust you.

Trainer 1: Look at me and see if you can get in touch with your suspicion.

Mike: (Long silence – tilts his head to one side, then to the other, looking at the trainer from different angles) I can't put my finger on it.

Trainer 2: I have a suggestion . . . go up and put your finger on him.

Mike: (Gets up from his chair and places one finger on the trainer's shoulder, but avoids looking at him)

Trainer 2: As you do that look into his face.

Mike: (Follows the suggestion) . . . I feel my suspicion fading.

Trainer 2: How did you lose your suspicion?

Mike: By looking into his eyes.

Commentary

By making contact at this simple level of touch, Mike found that the external world – in this case the trainer – was actually different from his internal picture. Having learnt this, Mike felt encouraged to discover more effective ways of making contact with others in the group.

This example illustrates one of the important benefits of co-training, and that is the improved capacity for working with projections (see Chapter 3). By having two or more trainers on the programme, course members are more likely to become aware of their projections – simply through paying attention to the differences he sees in them. For some course members the trainers can represent extremes e.g. good-Daddy and bad-Daddy.

By having two trainers at the same time the course member finds it easier to raise his concern about one of the trainers. (On this programme Mike had been quiet in the sessions which were led by trainer 1.) Having raised the issue it was much easier for trainer 2 to find an appropriate intervention because he was more able to remain detached from the process.

FEELINGS

This section is written in the first person, and from the personal viewpoint of one of the trainers. To highlight this, a different typeface is used. In addition, there are ongoing professional comments. There are two reasons for including this section; firstly, IRO invites people to explore their feelings (so often constrained in Western culture) and a third-person description does not portray this with sufficient power. Secondly the staff themselves use their own feelings as a principal guide to process interventions and personal process work, for example, 'I feel bored with you rambling on. What is going on with you?' or, 'I feel confused when you keep switching topics like that. Slow down and take it one item at a time.' Also the trainers use their feelings, without necessarily expressing them openly and directly to the person concerned.

Fear

Once I was scared, and yet fascinated and excited at the same time. Scared with the uncertainty, with the lack of direction, with the absence of predictability, with the power I had and seemingly didn't have. Scared by what I or my colleagues might say or do. Scared with the challenges of one-up, aggressive individuals, and the demands of 'hurry up' types to get moving, to do something worthwhile. And scared most of all with the silences, particularly those early uncomfortable ones near the beginning of the course. Oh, the relief when somebody else did or said something, and I honoured my commitment not to take on too much responsibility! Yet I and my colleagues carried on with the programme, fascinated and mesmerised. This fascination and excitement outweighed the fear most of the time. However, sometimes I would think: Why am I doing this? There must be easier ways to earn a living, easier ways of training people in interpersonal skills.

Gradually I discovered things, like the importance of silences and how they are broken, the fascination of the unpredictable, and most of all my own abilities to manage the uncertainty of direction and the ambiguity of the power relationship between myself and the group, and within different parts of myself. With time I understood more fully the apprehension and fear of many of the participants, invited into a situation alien to most of their educational experiences, with the possibility of finding out and sharing all sorts of things about themselves. Their fear at dropping tried and tested ways of doing things, however ineffective and even downright useless, scared to try out new things which might be contrary to all their learning and personal rules, and their boss's implicit demands of them, and their organisational cultures.

Handling fear is an important demand and responsibility for trainers involved in personal process work. Firstly, as far as his own scare is concerned, it may be worth talking about this openly with the group. Undoubtedly it is certainly important to discuss the source of the fear, e.g. a 'difficult' course member; stretching personal limits of competence too far; breaking your own rules; the activities and interventions of a colleague

Secondly, in terms of handling individual and group fear, offering protection is very important, for example, 'Go to the person who is safest for you to try this out'; 'If this is too risky for you, try something less risky'; 'What do you need to do so that you feel more comfortable here'; and 'Keep breathing deeply'.

Excitement

Excitement is often the other side of fear, and maybe one of the main attractions of personal process work to trainers and participants alike. The excitement when group members go actively looking for things. Excitement from the unknown, new learning, new directions, highs and lows, peaks and troughs, personal discoveries and revelations. The 'Ah! Ah!, now I understand' experience; and the energy, fun and closeness that can come from this excitement, even the impression of timelessness. The excitement of individuals realising that they don't have to be trapped by past rules or untested organisational demands. My excitement at their discoveries.

Personal learning can be uncomfortable, and it can also be exciting. This excitement needs the support of permission from the trainers, as well as protection so that people do not have fun at someone else's expense. By removing traditional and recognised structures from IRO, the uncertainty provided creates in itself opportunities for excitement. By the interventions they make, the trainers can help generate and harness excitement, e.g. 'Go round the group one by one and offer your feedback'; 'Be the castle you see yourself as. Describe yourself, starting with I am . . . . '; 'Find the excitement behind your anxiety'.

Boredom

Fields of boredom rolling into the distance, often half to two-thirds of the way through the programme. Not every programme, but when they occur for a minute or an hour, clearly this is the opposite of excitement. Energy draining, time dragging, frustrating. Is this a natural break, a plateau, a time for consolidation of learning? Or is this avoidance, evasions, signs of unfinished business in the group, or between the group and staff. Am I colluding in the boredom?

An important permission for the trainers to give course members is to encourage them to state whenever they are bored. Possible interventions by the trainers include; 'I'm bored and I imagine some of you are'; 'I don't think the group is making the best use of its time'.

Peace

Peace often comes with silences, sometimes long silences, towards the end of the programme. Peace, stillness and contentment, with the noises of the world outside the only sounds to intervene. Often part of a plateau after someone has done some important or intense work, or after a series of energetic exchanges and explanations. Those who felt they had to fill up the gaps in conversations have given up the rule, thank goodness. Sometimes someone works out how much the silence has cost the sponsoring organisations. But it gives me a break from the intensity, and many people remember the meditative periods as part of their learning. Some of them haven't had a moment of peace in years.

It is not unusual for participants to report that they are at peace with themselves for the first time for years. Often this peace is based on self-understanding and acceptance. One important intervention from the trainers is to encourage individuals to find ways of giving themselves peace after the programme is over, for example recreation, holidays, meditation and relaxation. A useful intervention from trainers is to explore with individuals what was happening to them during the moments of peace.

Anger

I used to be frightened of outbursts of anger, hostility and aggression.

I imagined it was my fault, that I'd done something wrong, or I was unreasonable in asking them to undertake this unstructured approach. Then I learnt it most often wasn't me, I didn't need to feel scared, or inadequate or hurt. Programme after programme, people bring in old angers (they've always been angry, they don't know how else to be) or new ones (anger at their boss and their organisation, anger and resentment at being sent on the course), anger at men, anger at women, and so on. Sometimes I get angry back – sometimes to collude and then become entrenched and sometimes to learn from the experience. Best is the explicitly angry man or woman – I know where I stand. Harder to handle is the elusiveness of sullen, passive hostility, and the deceitfulness of the 'I'm only being reasonable and logical' declarations. And what about my own anger? Do I share it and work it through, do I reject the individual concerned, do I seek counselling from one of my colleagues out of session? I'll take any of these options, depending on the support available.

One way or another, anger gets great support in our culture as a 'medium' for relating to people, particularly among men. Appropriate use of anger is a vital theme in interpersonal skills training generally and in personal process work in particular. Trainers act as temporary managers and surrogate authority figures, and are frequently the focus of left-over or generalised anger brought in by course members. It is clearly important for trainers to understand this projection process, and take care of themselves in the face of it. It is also important for personal process trainers to give permission to those 'angry men' who only use anger to find other ways of being, e.g. 'I notice you offer me repeated anger. Is there anything else you have to offer me?'; 'Is this a typical pattern for you, to get angry with quieter group members?'

It can also be important to invite those course members who seem excessively reasonable and tolerant to discover whether they have any buried anger (on the basis that unexpressed anger can be self-damaging). For example; 'You're smiling, and at the same time I imagine you're angry with what he just said to you'; 'What are the consequences for you of never getting angry, however much you've been put down'?

Warmth and closeness

The closeness of shared intimacy and shared feelings. The sharing of appreciations. Very often during the week, the room and the circle of chairs seems to get smaller and smaller. Most satisfying of all is the warmth and closeness that comes from those hostile, paranoid, suspicious, aloof and cold people finding out that it's okay for them to drop their defences and share good feelings with others. The surprise they get when they find out that they don't get hurt or exploited. The closeness and joy of seeing someone discard a personal rule that's limited their life and relationships. And the closeness and glow we trainers share after a good programme.

Great attention is paid to team spirit, team building, collaboration and co-operation in organisations. Most people see these as good things, essential to effectiveness at work. At the same time our culture sends opposite and interfering messages, e.g; Strive; Achieve; Get them before they get you; Be a winner and stay on top; Be aggressive!

These contradictions give a basis for many training interventions, e.g; 'What do you imagine will happen if you get close to someone here?'; 'Notice how often you have put people down in the group. No wonder they don't trust you'.

These are not the only feelings experienced on the course. Confusion, inadequacy, hurt, sadness, triumph, arrogance, guilt, cynicism, tiredness, satisfaction and joy all happen and play their part in the learning process.

OUTCOMES, CONSEQUENCES AND EFFECTIVE-NESS

Systematic analysis of the outcomes and effectiveness of feeling based interpersonal skills training programmes is notoriously difficult and complex. To a large extent this seems to be inevitable given the subjective and personal nature of feelings, and the divergent nature of the humanistic psychology principles on which these programmes are firmly based.

One indication of the difficulty of systematic analysis is that on occasions individuals have left the programme saying that the course was of minimal benefit and then have contacted us at a later date to report on the specific benefit that they have derived from the programme. However, there are some points of reference for monitoring the course.

As stated earlier, feedback is given as an integral part of the closing activities, and one of the tutorial team notes it down, in an abbreviated form. A typical example is shown in Table 4.7.

Most of the feedback is positive, and certainly any negative feedback is explored and responded to in various ways, ranging from rejection, through to the trainer doing some self-development, experimentation with style, or programme redesign. The feedback in Table 4.7 is full of good feelings. However, as is typical of end-of-course feedback, it does not give any reliable idea of what will happen to individuals after the programme.

Table 4.7
An example of feedback from one IRO course

---

1   I feel absolutely great now, although I felt uncomfortable at times.

2   I felt anxiety, appreciation and admiration. Thank you very much, all three. I felt particular affinity with . . .

3   All three of you have been extremely helpful to the whole group in different ways, but I think you could have put in more direction in the beginning.

4   One of the things I got out of the course was feedback on management skills as well as interpersonal skills. Thanks to you all.

5   I found you three complementary . . . More involved in first two days. On Monday I couldn't believe it would work, but found it immensely helpful.

6   Only course I've been on (and I've been on a lot) which I've enjoyed.

7   I've discovered that people are naturally warm and understanding. I just have to reach out.

8   I've thoroughly enjoyed the course and got a lot out of it.

9   I've got so much out of the course, and my particular thanks to . . .

10   I was clinging to the programme at the start of the week, but I've got so much out of it.

11   It has been a tremendous course – I've learnt so much.

12   I would like to thank . . . especially for his help.

13   You've made a superb effort to get this course working.

The staff also offer opportunities for ongoing contact at the end of the programme, by inviting the participants to take the initiative in telephoning, writing or visiting. Having helped people explore their relationships, it is very important that the trainers then do not sever contact. This crucial ethical issue is discussed in the next chapter. Suffice to say that nearly all this post-course contact is 'good news' in terms of positive experiences and post-course decisions as defined by the ex-participants. For example, a recent participant reported in conversation with one of the trainers that not only had the course helped him manage his relationships with his boss and one of his subordinates more effectively, but also stimulated him to undertake professional training with a view to furthering his career in the organisation. This typical example can be contrasted with another recent participant who had experienced a reduced self-confidence since returning to work, as reported by his personnel officer to one of the trainers. Fortunately such examples are rare, and in any event an offer of post-course counselling is made to help any individual who should require it.

It is also clear that ex-participants recommend others from their organisation, so that the course is currently very popular. Many individuals return to continue their personal learning on other, related courses. All these outcomes indicate, but do not 'prove', the effectiveness of the course for many people at an individual level. However, the impact on the sponsoring organisations is much less clear.

Based on the informal post-course feedback received, consequences for individuals range from:

1   Rejection of the experience and its validity. This is inevitable for a variety of reasons, and the purpose of the pre-course screening is to minimise the extent to which this happens.

2   Acceptance of the validity of the experience, without any change in behaviours, interpersonal styles or skills. The course becomes just a memory.

3   Change in styles and skills on a temporary basis, with eventual regression back to old patterns, particularly under pressure. To minimise this event, staff encourage participants at the end of the course to:

   (a)   Take a small step at a time with their new learning, being assertive e.g; 'Don't experiment with the biggest autocrat in your organisation'.

   (b)   Not to put pressure on themselves if experiments do not work the first time.

4   Change of personal styles and skills in small or large ways. Very occasionally, this leads to 'hurt' for others and the staff offer post-course support wherever feasible.

The majority of people attending the programme make changes that lead to increased self-understanding, a reduction in self-defeating behaviours and an increase in skills in relating to others.

Such changes are the whole point of the course. To verify its effectiveness more systematically and objectively, research has been carried out to evaluate the programme. Preliminary examination of the findings appear positive, and the results of the work will appear in the near future.

References

1   Barker, D.M. *T.A. and Training: The Theory and Use of Trans-actional Analysis in Organisations* Gower, 1980, Chapter 17.
2   As above, Chapter 10 p.80
3   Pfeiffer J.W. & Jones, J.E. *A Handbook of Structured Experiences*, vols. I to IV, University Associates, 1974–81.
4   Pesso A. *Movement in Psychology: Psychomotor Techniques and Training* University of London Press Ltd, 1969.
5   Bion, W.R. *Experiences in Groups*, Tavistock Publications, 1961.
6   Heron, J. *Co-Counselling Teachers*, British Postgraduate Medical Federation, 1978.

5
PROFESSIONAL AND ETHICAL ISSUES

Feeling-based training programmes, particularly those which involve personal process work, raise a number of professional and ethical issues. The nature of these issues is such that there are few obvious guidelines (e.g. the trainer decides that he will only take responsibility for 50 per cent of the learning – what does this mean in practice? Under what circumstances will he change his decision? Why not 55 per cent of the responsibility?). The issues dealt with in this chapter are the ones which we have considered to be most important in our work. The implications of these issues and how we attempt to manage them are also outlined. We do recognise, however, the need for each trainer to identify the issues and concerns which are important to him (and this will vary according to the type of programme he runs; the constraints of the organisations in which he works; his professional competence and abilities; the type of group with whom he works etc); and then to establish his own guidelines. In our experience the guidelines need to be continually monitored and modified by each trainer in response to each new training event.

PERSONAL CHANGE

The primary role of the interpersonal skills trainer is to facilitate changes in behaviour, feelings and attitudes. Even if someone only receives confirmation that his behaviour, feelings and attitudes are appropriate, that confirmation is a change in attitude and is likely to be accompanied by a change in feelings, e.g. more confidence. The starting point for such changes is the development of awareness. The decision for the change and the nature of that change can only be made by each individual. The principal consequence of this is that it is impossible for the trainer or anyone else, to predict or plan for specific behavioural outcomes from his work with any individual. It is likely that on most feeling-based programmes the chief aims will be met for most course members, namely:

1 Increase in self-confidence;
2 Wider repertoire of behaviour;
3 Increased willingness to express feelings;
4 Increased willingness to take responsibility for their own behaviour.

However, for some individuals this will not take place for a variety of reasons (e.g. resistance, fear, lack of trust, lack of support, inappropriate trainer interventions, feeling 'stuck' in infantile and inappropriate patterns of behaviour e.g. dependency). Even with individuals who accomplish these aims what the resultant changes mean in terms of their behaviour is very unpredictable. For example, an individual may explore his passivity through personal process work and then could make any one of the following decisions:

1 Not to change the nature or frequency of that behaviour (because he is satisfied being that way)
2 Choose to be passive more often (either because he is now aware of the benefits, to him, of his passivity *or* as his way of resisting change)
3 Choose to be less passive (i.e. take the initiative)
4 Choose to be assertive (because it is more personally rewarding)
5 Choose to be aggressive (as a way of discharging his unfinished business)
6 Choose to be manipulative (having discovered the power of his passivity in his relationship with others he can more purposefully exploit this part of himself)
7 Choose to be discriminating (having recognised that there are times to be passive, assertive, aggressive etc. and what is important is giving himself the freedom to choose how to be from moment to moment)

The consequence of encouraging the individual to take responsibility for his own behaviour is that the trainer cannot offer any absolute certainty about the specific outcomes of the training to either the course member or to the sponsoring organisation. Not only do we believe that the trainer needs to make this clear to both parties before the training event, but also that he needs to point out that some of the

outcome could be 'negative' (e.g. the course member loses confidence or feels 'stuck' in some way; he decides to change his job or leave
the organisation; he leaves the course with more confusion or
uncertainty than he arrived with etc). Such outcomes may be
short-term (one or two weeks) or of longer duration; and, for most
people who experience them, they are likely to be a continuation of the
learning process – albeit an uncomfortable one. A small minority of
those who leave a course in this way are only likely to learn from the
experience with additional support – such as the trainer, someone in
the organisation, or more specialised help. Again, the trainer needs to
indicate this possibility to both the course member and the sponsoring
organisation and to take appropriate action to make post-course
support available (see pp. 110–11).

These cautions are particularly necessary when either the course
member or the organisation have a clear expectation of behavioural
change (e.g. 'I want to stop being aggressive'), or where there is a
conflict of expectations (e.g. 'I want to be more assertive but my boss
wants me to be more compliant'). Within a training programme the
trainer can only work with the needs, expectations and perceptions of
the course member.

The uncertainty about outcomes has implications not only for the
course member and his organisation but also for his family and
friends. Whatever changes the course member makes they are
unlikely to be restricted to his work – they are going to affect,
sometimes more dramatically, his relationships with his family. Any
approach to interpersonal skills training, *particularly where it involves
personal process work*, will inevitably raise questions for each course
member about *all* of his relationships – both work and domestic – no
matter how narrow the objectives of the programme. For example, a
course member who develops assertive behaviour for use in the
organisation is likely to use the same behaviour in his family life. The
problem here is that the family is, invariably, excluded from any
contract-setting between the trainer, the course member and the
nominating organisation. They only become aware of the nature and
consequences of the training when the individual returns from the
course and they are having to respond to a new behaviour. The trainer
who believes, as we do, that he has some responsibility for managing
this process, can offer two interventions:

1   Prepare the course member for returning to his family – make
    him aware of their likely expectations (they probably want to
    say 'hello' to the person they said 'goodbye' to); their likely
    feelings (e.g. anxiety, uncertainty, jealousy, suspicion, hostil-
    ity etc.); how to talk about their experiences of the course (leave

the initiative with the other person, avoid jargon or evangelism, aim to include rather than exclude the other person in any discussion); and suggest that the best way of taking care of himself is by taking care of those who are important to him.

2   Offer post-course support – not only on work-related issues but also on domestic concerns. How far the trainer becomes involved in areas like family counselling before referring the individual to specialised services, will depend on the trainer, his experience, skill, willingness and availability. What is important, however, is that he clearly explains to each training group the type of post-course support, if any, he is willing to offer.

The more that trainers and organisations begin to move into feeling-based training programmes the greater, in our view, does the issue of the course member's family relationships become. One potential way for doing more in this important area is for both trainers and organisations to offer training events for couples – the course member and his/her spouse.

This issue brings into focus one of the basic concerns, in our experience, that people have about this form of training. This concern can be succinctly expressed in the question: What right does the trainer have to intervene in the lives of other people? Our response to this question is that the trainer does not have the right – any intervention he makes with an individual is dependent on that person's permission. Generally any person who chooses to attend training programmes grants that permission to the trainer – provided he wants to come and has some understanding of the nature of the event (see pp. 105–6). Within the programme each course member is choosing from moment to moment when to offer and refuse further permission to the trainer, e.g.

Trainer: What are you doing? (to someone who looks agitated)
Trainee: I don't want to talk about it
Trainer: O.K.

What the trainer needs to be aware of is that he can only effectively work with someone on the basis of their permission – attempts to push someone where they do not want to go will invariably lead to resistance and mutual bad feelings.

VALUES OF PERSONAL PROCESS WORK

The uncertainty about the specific outcomes of feeling-based programmes – beyond the broad aims mentioned earlier in this chapter – is a direct reflection of the values underlying this form of training. Some of the significant values have already been outlined in Chapter 3 (see pp. 42–3). A brief summary of these values is as follows:

1　Man is a whole who is (rather than has) a body, emotions, thoughts, sensations and perceptions, all of which function interrelatedly.

2　Feelings are an important dimension in relationships and generally should be expressed rather than repressed.

3　There are no right answers. Each person, who is by definition unique, must discover his own needs of others and how to satisfy those needs.

4　Learning can only take place when the individual is prepared to experiment with his behaviour.

5　Man is neither intrinsically good or bad. He does have the potential for change and growth.

Another value, not mentioned earlier, is:

6　Each person is responsible for his behaviour (both overt and covert); his feelings (e.g. other people do not make him angry, he chooses to be angry in response to them); and the limits he sets himself (e.g. values, rules, attitudes).

Because this form of training is so heavily based on values it raises a number of important issues. Firstly, the trainer needs to be clear in his own mind that his work is based on values and assumptions. These values reflect a way of looking at the world and human behaviour – other people have different values and see the world differently. Simply by having these values he is challenging not only individuals but also established views of the world – cultural, social, political and religious. Even in a pluralist society such as ours these values conflict with most of the prevailing ideologies. For example, at the political level the concept of personal responsibility conflicts with the collectivism of socialism and the emphasis on feelings attracts little sympathy from the exponents of the *laissez-faire* individualism of conservatism. The values confront the dangers of all ideologies and organisations by their insistence on accepting only those rules and values that make sense to each individual and by stressing the primacy of individual needs in preference to the real or imagined needs of others. At the very least the trainer can expect to have his values challenged or questioned. What this conflict of values can often mean is that individuals attending feeling-based programmes are having to cope with what they see as a confrontation to their way of seeing the world and, indeed, their purpose in life. For example, the Christian who believes in the concept of original sin is confronted with a training event which is based on the assumption that man is neither intrinsically good nor bad. The trainer, therefore, needs to be aware of the extent to which his values and interventions challenge individuals at all levels (personal, cultural, political, spiritual) and be prepared to offer appropriate support. This support will include such interventions as: stating clearly what his values are, offering them as values not facts, refusing to be dogmatic over a clash of values, being genuinely prepared to accept another's view of the world without giving up his own, being willing to find a way to work with an individual with whom he has such differences. Challenge without support is likely to lead to both parties taking up entrenched positions, each finding it impossible to work with and learn from the other.

The extent to which the trainer's values challenge the norms of our society can be quite dramatic. This drama is illustrated by the following example of a manager who recently attended a feeling-based programme. He was generally seen by the organisation as an effective, industrious manager who could benefit from improving his communication and his relationships at work. Some of the reasons for his perceived effectiveness were that he had strong rules about the need to do a perfect job; because, apart from the odd occasion, he did not express many feelings but went about his work and generally dealt with people in a 'rational way' (i.e. not obviously emotional or impulsive); and seemed to thrive on pressure. As a result of the programme the manager became aware of the costs to him and others (both at work and home) of his compulsive need for perfection and decided to approach tasks and people in a more discriminating way (e.g. he started telling his boss that some deadlines were unrealistic, that he wanted more involvement in setting objectives, he started taking the pressure for perfection off himself and others). He also learnt about the costs to him of repressing feelings (e.g. inflicting unexpressed feelings on to the wrong people, keeping his distance, sending out double messages etc.) and started experimenting with expressing his feelings (not in a dramatic or cathartic way). He also learnt about the costs to him, and others, (e.g. dissatisfaction, exhaustion, not listening, etc.) of putting himself under pressure and responding to the demands of others to accept pressure as a norm of organisational life. He, therefore, decided to resist self-imposed pressure and to question openly the organisational norm. Although he made the changes, achieved his goals, and perceived the quality of his work and his relationships to have improved, he was aware that in this process others saw him within the organisation as challenging rules of behaviour (although these were expectations rather than agreed rules) and, as a result, appeared to them as a less effective manager. The reason for this view was that the behaviours that he changed were ones that his organisation were encouraging (both explicitly and implicitly) in their employees. In this respect the organisation was reflecting the rules and values that our society has been, and still is, promoting in the home, in schools, in society, and in political life. These rules are often expressed in the form of slogans:

> Always try to do your best
> Get others before they get you
> To be emotional is to be weak
> Always work hard and be efficient
> Don't have fun

When the trainer challenges the individual about these and similar rules, encouraging him to be selective about responding to these demands, he is also confronting the organisation and the society.

It is our belief that when the trainer works in this way with individuals and organisations he needs to make clear statements to all parties about his values and the consequences of working with these values. To deny the values or to try and underplay them is dishonest. The consequence of such dishonesty is loss of credibility for the trainer and his work – at the simplest level he is not practising what he is preaching – with the course member, the sponsoring organisation, and, if independently employed, with his own organisation.

LIMITATIONS OF THE VALUES

The values described above are common to a number of approaches to personal process work and they derive from the movement now known as humanistic psychology. This movement started in the USA after the Second World War and grew out of the work of people like Abraham Maslow[1] and Carl Rogers[2]. Other important influences on the development of humanistic psychology were the T-group approach and Eastern religion and philosophy, particularly Zen Buddhism. The movement is sometimes referred to as the Third Force – behaviourism and psychoanalysis being the first and second forces, respectively. Humanistic psychology became particularly popular on the West Coast of the USA in the early 1960s through the work of such people as Will Schultz[3] (Encounter Groups) and Fritz Perls[4] (Gestalt therapy). Through the work of the Esalen Institute, particularly, there developed what is now generally known as the 'growth movement'. This coincided with the development of the 'hippy movement' and these two sub-cultures were soon to both influence and reinforce each other. Although, in retrospect, it can be seen that the economic crises and recessions of the 1970s dealt a severe blow to both these movements, there is little doubt that the excesses and indulgences of many of the people involved at that time had already seriously discredited them in the minds of some sectors of the public. One of the main problems with the early 'growth movement' was the belief (particularly prevalent in Encounter Groups) that anyone could set up and run training groups. This belief was carried over into interpersonal skills training when in the 1960s and early 1970s inexperienced trainers attempted to use Encounter Group exercises on their programmes. These early experiences still haunt interpersonal skills training and the people who attend programmes now are likely to have heard stories – real and apocryphal – that involve course members 'breaking down' because of psychological pressure.

A serious limitation, therefore, on the acceptance of both the values and the training experience stems from the evangelism and lack of discrimination of the earlier practitioners. Ironically, these early facilitators who subscribed to one of the basic values – each person is unique and needs to find his own answers – would run training events in which participants were coerced into activities like trust-building exercises (e.g. falling backwards into the arms of course members) or exercises which involved touching or being touched by other course members. *The pressure on people to break through their resistances, in this way, is the antithesis of the learning approach involved in personal process work as described in Chapter 3, where individuals are encouraged to stay with and discover more about the nature of their resistance.*

The other legacy of that time which still affects the credibility of feeling-based training is its association in the public mind with the hippy ethos. One of the consequences of the inter-relationship between the 'growth movement' and the 'hippy movement' was the popularising of the jargon initially associated with the former. Therefore, when trainers start using their jargon they can sound like superannuated 'flower children'. Typical words and phrases are: 'I am going to lay a trip on you'; 'It's OK to feel -' (sad, angry etc); 'How are you stopping yourself?'; 'What is going on with you?'; 'Take care of yourself'; 'Enjoy the experience' (to someone who is confused). The problem is that having acquired this jargon – and in the context of a training programme it can be an effective form of communication – the trainer either uses it (and then has to cope with individual reaction to it), or puts a great deal of energy (energy is another jargon word) into using equally simple language. The hippy association goes well beyond the use of language. The trainer needs to be aware of how easily his dress (jeans, sandals), his personal appearance (beards, moustaches, long hair) can fulfil the course member's stereotype. This particular stereotype – especially if the trainer encourages it, either consciously or unawares – can increase the level of confrontation between the trainer and the group, especially if the course members are not allowed to wear jeans and sandals to work!

Apart from guilt by association, the biggest limitation of these values is that they were developed in and for an affluent middle-class culture (the West Coast of America). This provenance is particularly evident in the notion of personal responsibility; i.e. I choose my behaviour and feelings – I can choose to be different. In the context of that culture unfettered choice appears to be self-evident. Individuals have the resources (financial and educational) and the freedom to use those resources to make realistic choices; e.g. to change jobs, stop working, get divorced, move house. Once that value is applied to a different environment; e.g. an unemployed youth in a depressed area, then the options for exercising choice are less apparent; e.g. I know I choose to be depressed but the fact that I am unemployed, have little money, little or no leisure facilities, inadequate housing, a poor education, no prospects and no mobility, can be seen as contributory factors to my depression. Even for people in an affluent middle-class culture freedom of choice is constrained by powerful social forces – sexual stereotyping, racial and ethnic pressures and barriers; remote political decisions such as a nuclear arms policy; laws and regulations; increasing restrictions on job opportunities and financial rewards. The trainer who subscribes to the value of personal responsibility needs to be aware of not only the real limitations on the exercise of choice (e.g. the individual cannot choose to live in a nuclear-free world) but also on the limitations imposed on an individual by the powerful force of social conditioning. For example, the woman who has spent thirty or more years learning how to be her daddy's coy little girl – and has received constant reinforcement for her choice – is unlikely to decide, in response to a few confronting interventions, that she can achieve more rewarding satisfaction by becoming assertive and autonomous. The pre-requisite for such a personal change would be a long-term helping relationship rather than a short course. Even the latter assumes some dissatisfaction with the way she is behaving now.

Often the trainer will encounter individuals whose behaviour he dislikes, disapproves of, or judges to be inappropriate. The reason for that reaction may well be that the individual concerned either consciously or without being aware of it, behaves in a way that refutes the trainer's values, e.g. does not believe that feelings are an important part of relationships, works on the assumption that he does not have choices etc. The danger on these occasions is that the trainer and/or the group can attempt to coerce or punish the 'renegade' course member. This can happen when either the trainer or the group choose to make their credibility dependent on the individual stepping into line, i.e. seeing the world in the same way. An important choice for the trainer in these circumstances is to ask himself what he can learn from the other person, i.e. what it is like to see the world through the other person's eyes.

A further limitation is that the values themselves, if realised, would presuppose a very different form of society. At the very least the new society would be based upon the maximum opportunity for personal choice and responsibility. The trainer who holds these values is quickly confronted with a need to define a role for himself in terms of exercising responsibility for changing society. One of the key activities of the trainer involved in feeling-based programmes is to offer a picture of a different, and better, future; e.g. it is possible to change behaviour, to satisfy needs. In the process of offering a vision of the future (for the individual, the group, the organisation, society) the trainer is also making a statement about his role in managing the transition. There are three roles to choose from:

1 *The revolutionary* – this role demands no less than the complete overturning of society, its institutions, its values and the generally acceptable codes of behaviour. The trainer may do this openly or covertly. Either way, the consequences of choosing this role are likely to be that he is both punished for, and punishing with, his behaviour; he is likely to suffer severe moods of depression and frustration; and is also likely to end up feeling ineffective or wasted. The main danger with this choice is that he can soon start seeing his work with individuals as a means to an end rather than as an end in itself. The chances are also that the people he works with are likely to experience him in the same way, i.e. they feel used.

2 *The doctor* – this role demands that the trainer accept the system he works in and sees that his responsibility is to equip individuals more effectively to adjust and cope. In crude terms he does a 'patch and repair job'. The likely problem with this role is that the trainer ends up totally exhausted and dispirited by the endless stream of 'casualties'. His patience and care are likely to turn into cynicism and rage.

3 *The evolutionist* – this role combines elements of both the 'revolutionary' and the 'doctor'. The trainer wants to change the system but his primary interest is in helping individuals to equip themselves. He realises that this means doing a number of 'patch and repair jobs' but he is also aware that he sometimes facilitates 'revolutions' in other people; i.e. they step willingly into their own future. Fundamental to this role is a willingness to accept people as they are rather than attempt to change them

to meet the expectations of the trainer. The long-term outcomes of his work – in terms of changing society – are always less important than his moment-by-moment contact with an individual.

Most trainers, in our experience, have a preference for one of these roles, or else flit, uncomfortably, between all three. The choice of role will have a crucial influence on how a trainer works with individuals and groups and on how he is seen by the organisation.

THE TRAINER

The role selected by the trainer provides some indication of an answer to a much more fundamental question. This question is: What does the trainer get out of personal process work? For many trainers the answer to this question is likely to be a complex one, because it probably embraces the satisfaction of a wide variety of needs. For example:

1 The opportunity to complete 'unfinished business' from childhood (e.g. becoming one of the powerful authority figures that he still has ambivalent feelings about – a mixture of attraction and repulsion). The 'unfinished business' could well be the prime motivation for choosing a career in one of the helping professions.

2 The opportunity to change other people as a way of avoiding having to change himself.

3 The opportunity to confront and overpower archaic fears; e.g. of being responsible for himself and others; of taking control; of managing uncertainty etc.

4 The opportunity to satisfy his curiosity about others and/or himself.

5 The opportunity to continue growing and learning.

6 The opportunity to satisfy needs for love, attention, recognition etc.

7 The opportunity to be rebellious and punitive.

8 The opportunity to take risks and achieve satisfaction from doing so.

9 The opportunity of establishing close relationships with a wide number of people.

10 The opportunity effectively to use and develop his skills of sensitivity and awareness.

Whatever the reasons, and the list above is not exhaustive, it is important for each trainer to be aware of the particular needs he is attempting to satisfy through his work. Any confusion, or lack of clarity, about his own needs is likely to create problems not only for himself but also for the people with whom he works. For example, the trainer whose basic need is to change other people as a way of avoiding having to change himself, is likely to be – and be seen by others as being – punitive, uncaring, hypocritical, and ineffective. This is one reason why we believe that it is a vital ethical issue for any trainer involved in personal process work to pay attention to his own training and development outside of the programmes he runs. *This commitment to his own development should be a continuing one and should involve him working at a higher risk level than any programme he runs.* For example, the appropriate training for the person working on feeling-based programmes would be provided in a therapy group where he has the opportunity to work on 'unfinished business' from childhood.

A second, and equally important, reason for undertaking this commitment is that when working with groups the trainer needs to model the behaviours and skills that he is encouraging his course members to develop. At the simplest level modelling involves sharing his values, as described earlier in this chapter, paying attention to and expressing feelings, using his awareness of himself and others as the basis for making interventions and taking risks by experimenting with his behaviour. In addition, he needs to be clear about his own boundaries with others; i.e. to know where he stops and others begin, so that he can achieve the necessary balance between involvement and detachment. The only way in which he can effectively develop and maintain these skills is through working on his own internal process. Although there are many ways of achieving this (e.g. peer supervision and feedback, feedback from course members, one-to-one counselling and therapy), it is important that a central part of the trainer's development involves being a member of a training group. Without that experience he will not fully appreciate the problems and difficulties of his own course members.

The extent to which the trainer can model these behaviours is limited in two ways. Firstly, by the limits he consciously imposes. For example, he may make a decision early in a programme not to express fully his anger at an individual because his judgement is that such an intervention is likely to be too high a risk for himself, the individual and/or the group to cope with at that stage. In this situation he may choose to ignore the individual or may choose to make a lower level intervention, e.g.

1 What are you doing? (addressing the individual)
2 I don't like what you are doing (addressing the individual)

The second limitation is beyond the trainer's immediate control and that is his degree of awareness at that particular time. All trainers, when working with groups, will discover times when they are out of touch with themselves and their feelings. Such moments will occur when individuals in the group present issues which are also unresolved for the trainer and he becomes confluent (i.e. confuses his boundaries) with their process; when the trainer is invited successfully by a course member into old compulsive patterns of behaviour (e.g. trying to be perfect); or when he is feeling tired. The important thing for the trainer to remember at such times is to *give himself permission to be confused, out of touch, behaving in old ways etc*. For in the process of accepting how he is at that time and giving himself permission to be that way, he is still modelling to the group and he is also likely to learn more about himself as well. The trainer who works with high expectations of himself (e.g. I need to be constantly aware on every occasion) is likely to experience many difficult occasions on programmes because he is diverting so much energy into monitoring himself that he actually misses important events that are happening with individuals and the group. The other problem for such a trainer is that he is likely to have equally high expectations of course members and they will either mirror his process (and end up experiencing their own failures) or they will resent and rebel against him.

TRAINING OF TRAINERS

Having identified the need for the continuing training and development of trainers involved in personal process work, it is necessary to ascertain what form that training should take. At the time of writing there is no professional body specifically for such trainers, nor any recognised form of training and qualification. Anyone can offer themselves as an interpersonal skills trainer and attempt to run feeling-based programmes. The only constraint on this situation is the willingness of organisations to employ them. The existing qualifications of professional bodies such as the Institute of Personnel Management or the Institute of Training and Development do not, in our opinion, qualify trainers to run feeling-based programmes. Both bodies offer broad-based courses for personnel officers and trainers respectively. There are a few specialised institutions (see Chapter 6 for more details) such as the Institute of Transactional Analysis which offer appropriate training and qualifications for those trainers who want to specialise in that particular approach. There are two important reasons for this absence of formality in the training of trainers. The first reason is that humanistic psychology embraces a large number of different approaches (TA, Gestalt, Encounter etc.)

not all of whom provide recognised professional training. The second reason is because of a value shared by many of these approaches, which is that the individual should be the primary, if not the only, assessor of his own competence and ability. Many training programmes in this area place equal emphasis on peer assessment. This means that each individual must take the responsibility for deciding when he is competent to engage in such work. We too accept this view. Irrespective of what training, qualifications, or experience, an individual has he is ready to engage course members in personal process work when he feels secure enough to take that risk. Our own experience leads us to believe that the individual who is seriously thinking of working on feeling-based programmes is more likely to be able to make that decision when he has:

1 At least two years' experience of interpersonal skills training at the thinking/doing levels.
2 Spent at least 100 hours as a member of a personal growth group.
3 Specialised knowledge and experience of one of the approaches to feeling-based learning.
4 Has worked, or is working, with a peer group of interpersonal skills trainers.

Having offered these guidelines, we are clear that our decision to work with another trainer on a programme like *Interpersonal Relationships in Organisations* would be more determined by:

1 The quality of the relationship with him/her.
2 The level of trust and openness in the relationship.
3 Common understanding of aims and range of interventions.
4 Mutual acceptance of differences in approach.
5 His/her level of awareness and openness to learning.

TRAINING AND THERAPY

Feeling-based programmes occupy a grey area between training and therapy. Those trainers who engage in personal process work on their programmes soon discover that there is no clear line of demarcation between the two approaches, there are merely differences of emphases. The reason for this is that both training and therapy are concerned with helping the individual to understand who he is and how he can cope more effectively with his environment. It is only by emphasising the extremes in both approaches that the trainer can begin to set some guidelines for himself. The important characteristics that emerge from looking at the extremes are:

Personal process work	*Therapy*
1 Is developmental and is firmly based on the assumption that course members are not 'sick' in any way but have the capacity for growth and learning.	1 Is curative, clients are unable to cope effectively with their lives and need specialist assistance in order to cope.
2 The trainer facilitates learning primarily through giving responsibility for that learning to each course member. The trainer's expertise and knowledge is freely shared with the course member.	2 The therapist clearly keeps for himself the role of expert and exercises more responsibility for learning. His expertise and knowledge may, or may not, be freely shared with the client.
3 The contract between both parties is short-term – ususally no more than one week.	3 The contract between both parties is likely to be long-term. It may involve an agreed number of sessions over a period of time – it may last for years.
4 Course members are encouraged to be autonomous from the start of the contract. Any form of dependency is actively discouraged by the trainer.	4 Although autonomy is the desired outcome there is likely to be an acceptance by both parties that there will be a period of dependency. Indeed, working through this dependency is often a key part of the learning process.
5 Learning will be focused on current problems in the course member's life (e.g. how to be assertive) and on what action he can take now in order to cope more effectively. Part of the learning may involve exploring historical issues but only in the context of how those issues are important now.	5 Learning will often be focused on historical problems in the client's life (e.g. his relationship with his father). Some therapists may also consider what choices the client has to work with these issues now – but not necessarily. In general, the emphasis is on the past as a way of understanding the present.
6 The desired outcomes are to increase awareness and skills for dealing with the present.	6 The primary objective is likely to be that through an improved understanding of the past the client can come to terms with the present and then increase awareness and skills.

By polarising the approaches in this way we are aware that some of the characteristics apply more clearly to particular forms of therapy (e.g. psychoanalysis) than others (e.g. Gestalt and TA as personal approaches to therapy are much closer to the characteristics of personal process work). What is important, however, is that the trainer who works with the training model described above, is more able to set and manage the boundary between training and therapy for himself and his groups. He does need to remember that irrespective of how well he manages the boundary his work is likely to be seen as a form of therapy by course members and organisations. This perception is likely to arouse extreme reactions (e.g. fear; hostility; cynicism and scorn; 'amateur psychologist'). When this occurs the trainer needs to intervene at the process level; e.g. 'What do you imagine will happen to you?'; 'What are you afraid of?'; 'What limits can you set for yourself?'; rather than at a content level e.g. 'Let me explain what I see as the differences between training and therapy'.

RESPONSIBILITIES OF THE TRAINER ON FEELING-BASED PROGRAMMES

Having identified some of the key professional and ethical issues in this area it is important to identify some of the responsibilities the trainer needs to exercise in his contact with training groups. These responsibilities begin before the start of a course.

Before the course

In our experience most people who attend feeling-based programmes do so from essentially a passive position. Someone in the organisation is likely to nominate them for the programme (with or without any discussion with them) and the individual accepts the nomination. In this situation the individual's reaction could be one, or more, of many – overt hostility, grudging acceptance, curiosity, excitement, fear, caution, happiness at the prospect of a week's holiday, suspicion, anger, feelings of failure, feelings of recognition. For most management and interpersonal skills training programmes the trainer accepts, albeit despairingly, that he is likely to be presented with groups offering this spectrum of reactions and that he is going to have to work hard to influence the orientation of the group. On feeling-based programmes such stoical acceptance is neither in the interest of the trainer, the individuals, or the organisation – the group could spend the first three days of the programme re-assessing expectations and understandings of what they are going to do in the last two days.

In order to overcome (or at least moderate) this eventuality the trainer needs to intervene in a number of ways before the programme starts. Firstly, to ensure that detailed notes are sent to nominators (these notes describe the nature of the programme, the learning method, the type of outcomes – both positive and negative and the importance of voluntary attendance). A copy of these notes should also be sent to the nominees some weeks in advance of the programme (see also Chapter 4). The trainer should then make direct contact with each nominee (either by telephone or in person) to:

1 Check the individual's understanding of the programme (although it is impossible in this way fully to prepare the individual for the experience, at least the trainer has alerted him to some of the chief possibilities, i.e. it is going to be different, he will have to take responsibility, he may find it uncomfortable, etc.).

2 Check his willingness to attend the programme (for most people their willingness is unlikely to be total – at best it will be tempered with apprehension. However, it is usually possible to detect a totally inappropriate nomination. In such circumstances where the trainer and nominee agree about the unsuitability of the programme the trainer then needs to contact the nominator to talk about alternative training programmes).

3 Begin the process of orienting the course member to the programme by asking him to identify the type of needs he can explore during the course. For example, he may have received feedback from someone in the organisation that he sometimes appears to be aggressive. Although the needs that are identified at this stage may in reality be cosmetic – saying more about the individual's perception of himself, or lack of it – he is beginning to focus on the learning possibilities for himself.

Although these interventions by the trainer do not, and should not, resolve all the problems of individuals coming to terms with feeling-based programmes, they do screen out some of the more inappropriate nominations.

During the course

One of the most important responsibilities that the trainer needs to manage in his contact with course members (before, during and after the course) is that of confidentiality. Whatever emerges from his contact with the individual must be treated as confidential. Although the sponsoring organisation pays for the training, the trainer's primary loyalty on feeling-based programmes must lie with the course member. The major reasons for maintaining confidentiality is that in order for people to learn on these programmes – to disclose information about themselves, to experiment and take risks with their behaviour, to give and receive feedback – they need to have some fixed boundaries of safety and security. The one certainty that the trainer can offer is that whatever happens in the group will remain the property of the group. Not only should the trainer explicitly make the offer on his part to the group, but should demand of the group their agreement to maintain a similar confidentiality about each other. The group should not be constrained from reporting back on their experiences of the trainer or the programme, but on their experiences and perceptions of other course members.

The trainer needs to make his position on confidentiality clear to both the individuals and the sponsoring organisations at the time of nomination. Failure to do so will lead to problems both during and after the programme (e.g. trying to develop trust with course members at the start of the programme, having to deal with demands from organisations about reports on individuals afterwards). Even after making a clear statement to this effect the trainer can still find himself under pressure to breach confidentiality. For example, a course member who has experienced some difficulties with the programme may well, on his return to the organisation, severely criticise the trainer and/or the programme as being ineffective. On hearing this the nominator may then contact the trainer to discuss the individual's feedback about the programme. Any such discussion needs to be managed in general terms – the trainer's perception about the programme, typical learning outcomes (both positive and nega- tive), the end-of-course feedback statements (anonymously) – other- wise the trainer can, in the very natural process of trying to defend himself from attack, breach confidentiality.

There are occasions – and these are rare in our experience – when the behaviour of an individual on a programme causes particular concern to the trainer. For example, an individual is carrying around a disproportionate amount of undischarged aggression which, in the trainer's perception, is likely to be turned inwards (suicide) or out onto other people. The warning signs for the trainer of such an individual are likely to include one, or more, of the following: exaggerated and frequent non-verbal behaviour (e.g. fist-clenching, banging chair, leg, other parts of body, eye-rolling etc); frequent statements about his difficulties in coping with himself and/or the programme; general agitation and tenseness both in session and outside programme time; difficulties in eating, sleeping; difficulties in making contact with other course members outside session; keeping himself isolated outside of session; dysfunctional behaviour in the group (e.g. stepping out of line so that he ends up being punished or experiencing bad feelings – confusion, inadequacy etc); frequent lapses of memory and failure to understand simple messages. In this situation the trainer's options are fairly limited; they are:

1   Talk to the individual about the problem with a view to his leaving the programme. If this is the decision then the trainer needs to offer himself as the contact between the individual and the organisation. On behalf of the individual the trainer needs to say to the nominator that both parties have agreed that this particular programme is unsuitable.

2   Talk to the individual about the problem, with a view to informing him about the specialised helping services that are available. In this situation the trainer can do no more than encourage the individual to see his local GP as the first contact point. For the trainer to do more in such circumstances (e.g. referring the individual to a therapist) is to both run the risk of exacerbating the problem and to exceed his level of responsibility and competence (and, indeed, to leave himself open to litigation).

In extreme situations, e.g. a course member being physically violent to another person on the programme, the trainer needs to tell that person to leave. The support, if any, that the trainer offers to the violent course member in these circumstances (e.g. post-course counselling, acting as mediator with the organisation) is a matter for personal choice. In these circumstances, we believe, the trainer's primary responsibility is to protect the rest of the group. If this protection means breaching confidentiality with that individual then that is one of the consequences he has to manage.

The trainer also has to pay attention to the need to offer protection to individuals when they are subjected to group pressure. It is quite common, in our experience, for groups to quickly develop norms of behaviour for themselves. For example, a common norm is for each person to take his turn in the 'hotseat' and engage in personal process work. Such pressure can be seen explicitly in the formal group – members ganging up on an individual demanding that he take some action. This pressure is also applied outside the formal programme, with individuals being set up for the next session. The ways in which the trainer can offer protection to the individual in these circumstances is by:

1   Checking with the individual what he wants to do at such times, e.g. 'What do you want for yourself?'

2   Giving the individual permission not to engage in personal process work, e.g. 'It's OK not to push yourself'.

3   Confronting the group process or course members who are exerting pressure, e.g. 'What's your interest in Bill doing this?'

How the individual responds to this form of group pressure is obviously an area for personal learning. The problem for the trainer and the individual concerned in pursuing this issue at that time is that both end up meeting the expectations and demands of the rest of the group. A better choice for the trainer is to confront the individuals who are setting the expectations and demands.

Another area where the trainer needs to exercise responsibility is where the group becomes too intense about learning. This situation is sometimes described as 'hot-housing'. The group seem unable to switch off – whether in session or out – and every moment has to be one of intense learning and/or catharsis. The very intensity drains energy, rather than generates it, and unless the trainer intervenes, the group can very soon exhaust itself. Some interventions the trainer can make to break up this process are:

1   Give the group some 'time-out' from the programme with some strong recommendations that they interrupt the process and spend time on their own or in doing some physical activity, e.g. walking, swimming, table-tennis etc.
2   Introduce a structured activity whose main aim is to offer course members an opportunity to have fun (e.g. a three-legged race) or to relax (e.g. a guided fantasy or breathing exercise).
3   Introduce a formal theory session that invites course members to switch out of feeling into thinking.

'Hot-housing', when it occurs in groups, is a seductive process for both the trainer (i.e. he has many opportunities to 'perform' in doing process work) and the course member (i.e. the very intensity of an intimate experience). The problems of energy loss and the natural reluctance to let go of the intensity far outweigh the benefits in our experience.

Even in programmes where the group fails to reach this level of intensity the trainer needs to be aware of that strange sense of euphoria that can occur for some individuals. This sense of euphoria usually develops when individuals are experiencing, perhaps for the first time, a heightened sense of well-being, acceptance (of self and others) and of intimacy. Typical behaviours associated with this state are – dilated pupils, broad smiles, slow and deliberate movements of the body and the use of religiose words; e.g. magical, spiritual, heavenly etc.

Another manifestation of this sense of euphoria stemming from heightened awareness is the experience or incidents that can loosely be described as 'paranormal'. Examples of these experiences are; unexpected flashes of insight or self-understanding; penetrating intuition about another person that the believer 'knows' to be true; anticipating correctly what another person is going to say etc. These experiences are not the sole preserve of course members but also occur to the trainer.

To experience this sense of euphoria is to see the world in a new way and to believe that anything is possible. Unfortunately this euphoric state is likely to be followed by an equally intense feeling of depression – usually the day following the course when the support he has enjoyed from the group is no longer available. To offer some guards against this occurring, the trainer, particularly in the last day of the programme, needs to encourage the course members to find ways in which they can let go of their experiences together. There are three interventions that can be made on the last day of feeling-based programmes to encourage this process (see Chapter 4 on IRO). They are:

1 Offering guidelines on how course members can take care of themselves after the programme (e.g. identifying some of the potential problems and experiences they may encounter; the need to develop support systems for themselves; how they can apply their learning etc.)

2 Offering them an opportunity to plan and talk through in small groups how to apply a particular item of learning (e.g. identifying important first steps, how to support their learning)

3 Allocating at least one hour for the group to say their goodbyes to each other and the trainers (this may take the form of offering specific appreciations and/or resentments; offering an item of feedback; shaking hands etc.). In our experience the groups that can more effectively manage the process of saying goodbye are more able to manage the process of saying hello to the people they meet on return.

After the course

Earlier in this Chapter (see p. 92) it was suggested that the trainer should make clear statements to the group about the nature, if any, of the post-course support he is prepared to offer. The support offered by any trainer will be determined by his willingness, his availability, as well as by whatever rules and values he has about personal process work; e.g. the trainer who is prepared to exercise more than 50 per cent responsibility for the learning on the programme is more likely to be pro-active about offering support (e.g. taking the responsibility to contact on a regular basis previous course members). While the trainer who believes his responsibility for the learning ends with the formal sessions will actively discourage any form of post-course contact because he thinks that in doing so he is encouraging dependency.

The guidelines that we have developed for ourselves in this area are:

1 The need to make a clear statement to each group about our willingness to respond to their request to make contact. In all cases the initiative must lie with the course member. (We do not have the resources for being pro-active.)

2 We will respond to any initiative made by the course member (e.g. by telephone, post, or personal contact). This may be at the level of giving a book reference, suggesting some particular reading or further training experience, talking about his experiences on the programme or following the programme.

3 If we detect any signs of dependency then the best choice (for both parties) is to confront the process.

4 If the request made is particularly demanding (e.g. a protracted counselling arrangement) then there is a need to agree a formal contract with that individual and/or his organisation. Again, this is to provide some safeguards for both parties.

Having established these guidelines it is possible for the trainer to enjoy post-course contact rather than endure it as some onerous responsibility. In addition to such contact providing the trainer with longer-term feedback about the effectiveness of his programmes, it is also one of the rich sources of reward available to him in working on feeling-based programmes.

References

1 Maslow, Abraham *Motivation and Personality* Second edition, Harper & Row, 1970.
2 Rogers, Carl *On becoming a Person* Constable, 1961.
3 Schutz, Will *Joy: Expanding Human Awareness* Penguin, 1961.
4 Perls, Frederick *The Gestalt Approach & Eyewitness to Therapy* Bantam, 1976.

6
PERSONAL
DEVELOPMENT

This final chapter is concerned with the personal development of the trainer, an area which is essentially the foundation for all the skills we have described so far in this book. We believe that if the trainer does not grow and develop and pay attention to his own well-being and training, then his effectiveness will diminish and he will be less able to help others grow and develop. So simply at the level of practising what he preaches, personal development has to be the highest priority for a trainer. Our main aim in what follows is to describe what we have discovered to be important for ourselves; allied to this we wanted to provide some starting points for the reader so that he can pursue his own training and development in a variety of ways. For this reason, a list of resources is given at the end of the chapter.

THE NEED FOR PERSONAL DEVELOPMENT

Over the years we have become increasingly aware that interpersonal skills training can be regarded as one of the helping professions. In this context the work can be demanding for two principal reasons. Firstly, some of the participants may well be in some distress and require special attention. The source of this distress for an individual could be a realisation that he is unlikely to progress further in his career; or an inability to cope with increasing demands placed on him both at work or at home. The course may even have been chosen as a last resort by the participant and/or his organisation. Being aware that these issues exist the trainer will probably offer a great deal of care and attention. The situation can be tiring for the trainer especially if the course member is endlessly making demands (e.g. for out-of-session counselling) or chooses to be angry and resentful as a cover for some underlying feelings of fear or sadness.

Secondly, the relationship between the trainer and trainee is often transient. During a week, or perhaps a slightly shorter or longer period of time, a sufficiently strong and trusting relationship has to be developed so that personal process work can take place. The trainer will need to play his full role in establishing this relationship, do his job and then find some way of saying goodbye and closing the relationship so that he is sufficiently 'finished' to be ready to greet the next group.

Against this background we discovered, as for example social workers often do, that emotional and physical exhaustion could be a serious problem; this process has been called 'burn-out'. Some of the symptoms of such exhaustion which we noticed were:

1 Lack of clarity over boundaries. This could lead to the trainer putting himself under too much pressure to succeed, confronting the group too hard and getting into a fruitless game of pressure and resistance. Equally, it might lead to letting too much go by; here the trainer feels he cannot be bothered, consequently reducing the number of process interventions he makes and thus appearing to be uninterested and withdrawn. The group may then exclude him, leaving him feeling even more tired and unappreciated.

2 An emotional see-saw, consisting of sudden bursts of energy, being followed by extreme lethargy. Sometimes the first sign of this is where the trainer uses all his energy at work and then comes home feeling depressed. Associated with this the trainer may store up his 'bad' feelings and unleash them at home, e.g. he expresses anger at his wife, rather than the difficult course member. (Families need time, attention and caring too.)

3 A general underlying anxiety, possibly leading the trainer to start worrying about everything, everyone and every minute detail. This in itself becomes an energy drain, for example, when time is then spent reviewing the handouts rather than spending five minutes relaxing!

With any of these symptoms there is the distinct possibility of a vicious circle where, for example, mental exhaustion leads to physical exhaustion, the physical exhaustion lowers resistance to illness and illness leads to mental exhaustion.

Before going on to describe what we found useful in dealing with some of these problems, we describe two remaining aspects of the job which can be sources of delight or despair.

A primary source of satisfaction in interpersonal skills training, and personal process work in particular, is helping individuals and groups see the world in a different and more rewarding way. Here there is scope for dramatically increasing the effectiveness of an organisation, especially when dealing with in-company groups. However, sometimes the organisation's culture remains untouched and if this is one of win/lose competition, scoring points, not expressing feelings of warmth, including perhaps an underlying fear (e.g. of redundancy, not getting promoted, being made a fool of) then the trainer may find that he has given much more than he has received in, for example, appreciation, attention and support.

A second and related point is the challenge of the job, particularly in terms of the high degree of concentration it requires at the levels of content and process. Each situation he deals with is likely to be different, with a number of questions to be considered moment by moment (e.g. 'How can I offer support to this person?'; 'What do they *really* want?'; 'Shall I intervene or not?'; 'I wonder what my colleague has in mind?'; 'Shall I introduce an exercise?'). This uncertainty can be very exciting, providing a 'high', especially where creative decisions are rapidly made and prove to be right. Yet, as with any challenging job, there can be times when it is too demanding and the trainer needs some respite. The need can be felt particularly strongly at the end of the course when the trainer is waiting for the group to prepare its review feedback. Indeed, there are probably few occupations where the person so frequently and consciously puts themselves up for judgement, these judgements usually being made by relative strangers.

So, it has been to counteract such 'negative' aspects of our work that personal development has been of prime importance, and what follows are some of the key points we have learned. They are grouped under two headings, 'Formal learning' and 'Informal learning'. These titles are not precise but by formal learning we mean things we have learned through specific training and therapy events; by informal learning we mean things we have learnt, and indeed continue to learn, on-the-job through insight, reflection and feedback.

FORMAL LEARNING

Between us we have experienced many types of interpersonal skills training and as our interest in personal process work has grown we have found it more and more necessary to pay particular attention to two closely related areas. These are firstly, increasing self-knowledge and secondly, physical and emotional well-being.

Increasing self knowledge means learning more about how we became who we are. There are many ways to do this (see the list of resources below) but for us Gestalt and TA have been particularly valuable. Through these we discovered such points as: how our past experiences could directly affect the choices we made with course members; the feelings we did, and did not, allow ourselves; the ways we competed with each other; the types of course members we might collude with. Some of the discoveries were painful and took some months, even years to assimilate; others were joyous revelations of new skills, new feelings, and happy, but long-forgotten memories. We rarely attended the same training event together, but we were quickly able to translate our learning, confusion, anxiety, curiosity and excitement back to our work and our relationships. We each learnt through observing the leaders of the various groups we went to; perhaps identifying with some of them too strongly before, in time, establishing our own individual identities. Other key influences on us, apart from Gestalt and TA have been the 'T' group[1], Encounter[1], Psychodrama[1], and Structural Integration (Rolfing); each revealing itself in our work to a greater or lesser extent.

Our physical and emotional well-being has been particularly affected by 'Rolfing' (see Human Potential Resources, p. 124). This is a form of especially penetrating massage, often unblocking deeply held emotions. Through this channel has come greater self-knowledge, but also more sensitivity to the body and non-verbal behaviour – one's own and others! Outside the context of formal learning we discovered some simple yet important ways of looking after ourselves, particularly with regard to physical and emotional well-being. These are dealt with in the next section, but before doing that we will give some basic guidelines that the reader can use in 'shopping around' for personal development groups and programmes.

1   Intuition can be crucial in assessing whether a particular leader or group is likely to be productive. Sometimes trust and liking can be much more important than any one technique or philosophy. Having said that, people can often learn a lot from somebody with whom they feel a little uncomfortable. This person may challenge and confront key issues. Liking can lead to collusion and an avoidance of conflict.

2   Obviously it is important to find out the cost and length of the commitment required.

3   Some groups and group leaders may implicitly encourage

dependency. As a *very* rough guide we would say that there is something wrong if the client is working on the same issues having been in a weekly group for more than a year.

4 Each person will need to make his own decision about how important it is that the group should be run by somebody with a professional qualification. For some clients intuition may be more important. Nevertheless, it is probably worth finding out the leader's attitude to professional qualifications and the basis on which he/she feels competent to run groups.

5 It is helpful if the prospective client is as clear as he can be about his needs. Indeed, he may want to approach the training/ therapy on a contract basis: 'This is what I want from you; this is what I'm prepared to offer'.

6 Some approaches take a strong individual focus, others a group focus and others a mixture. Each client can make guesses about how comfortable he/she would be in the light of these general training styles.

7 Some methods reinforce the client's learning style, others present a direct challenge. If the client is feeling completely stuck then he might want to go to a trainer/leader whose approach is markedly different from what he is used to, e.g. if the client finds it easy to conceptualise and analyse then some 'bodywork', such as Rolfing, might well be more productive.

8 As a broad generalisation groups thrive where the members are pro-active almost to the point of selfishness in terms of looking after their own needs and actively looking for learning.

INFORMAL LEARNING

This section is concerned with how the trainer can pursue his own internal processes and the way in which he puts himself under pressure. Here are some of the pressures we have put ourselves under:

I must do everything perfectly all the time.
I must do everything in a hurry.
I must be loved by everybody.
I must please everybody and never say 'no'.
If I knew everything I would be omnipotent.
I must look after the world.
If things go wrong it must be my fault.
There is always a perfect solution to every problem.
When my ideas are rejected I am being rejected.
I must never express my feelings.

The trainer can help to alleviate such pressures by giving himself permissions: a general permission of self-acceptance ('It's OK to be who I am') and a specific permission related to the particular source of internal pressure (e.g. 'It's OK for me to make mistakes from time to time; I don't have to be perfect'). Anyway, it does not make sense for a trainer to be harder on himself than he is on his course members. We found it was important to give each other such permissions.

Managing anxiety

We mentioned earlier points such as organisational culture, transient relationships and putting oneself up for judgement. These and other factors can create anxiety in the trainer. In managing our anxiety we have found it valuable, for all of us, to accept its legitimacy. If we start saying to ourselves 'I must not feel anxious', then this is likely to increase our anxiety. Along with this self-acceptance we believe it is important that the person supports himself physically (sitting upright, feet on the floor and breathing deeply). Having done this, it will be easier to put energy outwards in terms of expressing feelings and managing the structure of the session, or showing a caring attitude. This way of centring (i.e. emotional and psychological stability) takes a little time. Seeking to rush through a potentially painful experience led us only to increased anxiety.

Experimenting with behaviour

Old patterns of behaviour can get in the way of the trainer's development where they lead him to limit his options in managing relationships. Allied to the internal pressure referred to above (e.g. 'I must be liked by everybody') the trainer may have an established training style which undercuts his effectiveness, (e.g. he stops himself from giving any type of negative feedback). He can explore this part of himself by experimenting with his behaviour. In doing this the following points will probably be helpful.

Any experiment is more likely to be successful if it constitutes a small step. Following on from the previous example this would mean offering odd 'small' items of negative feedback. If too large a step is taken (perhaps going from one extreme to the other) then the greater the chance of the person's worst fears being realised, e.g. the negative feedback, because it was expressed too strongly, is totally rejected and the trainer ends up feeling 'bad' (perhaps depressed) for having broken a rule which may have its origins in childhood. The breaking of such a rule can lead to a backlash where the experimenter feels just like a child having disobeyed an important authority figure (e.g. mother or father) on a really important issue.

It is for this reason that the small step should be accompanied by discrimination and reward. Discrimination means taking care about who is the object of the experiment. It would not be wise for the person to experiment with giving negative feedback to the individual in the group who is most likely to over-react and reject. Rewards should accompany the experiment whether it is successful or not. The reward is for breaking the old pattern, regardless of the outcome. Just as the old rule was probably learnt through certain rewards and punishments, so the new rule needs to be reinforced. What constitutes a suitable reward will obviously vary from individual to individual: for one person it could simply mean making a mental note of it and feeling good about having tried something different; for somebody else a tangible reward (such as buying oneself something) could be important.

What can happen is that the person sabotages himself either *before* the event (i.e. stops himself from experimenting – 'It's not really important') or *afterwards* ('What I did wasn't a *real* test'). With a little thought people can usually identify their 'favourite' way of sabotaging themselves and thus be ready to counteract it.

Managing the group

When the group starts assembling, the trainer has many options in terms of the energy he puts into acting as a 'host', trying to put people at their ease and helping conversation along. As a way of husbanding his energy the trainer generally would do well to let the participants carry their fair share of the socialising. If the trainer overplays the role of host it may be too sharp a contrast with the rest of the programme which is based on the assumption that the group will 'make most of the running'. Obviously there are exceptions. It may be that, for example, he suspects a particular group may be difficult in some way and he may then, as part of a strategy of looking after himself, want to make contact with the group quickly so that he can get some idea of their attitudes and orientation to the programme. Once the programme is underway then the trainer is faced with decisions about how much time and energy he invests in particular individuals and the group. In the light of these decisions he will then make process interventions. In this context we have found the following points are worth remembering:

1   The trainer cannot *make* people trust him. In the end all he can do is be 'straight' about himself and his values and it is up to others whether they trust him or not.

2   It is not solely up to the trainer to earn trust. Trust is a two-way process and the course members themselves will not always be people whom the trainer can trust. On occasions the trainer may want to make this clear. 'I am finding it difficult to trust you because . . . '

3   The trainer cannot *make* people learn. He can only make offers which may or may not be accepted.

4   The success of a course should not be measured on the basis of 'getting through' to everybody. The trainer has several options in handling the person who rejects and/or does not understand; the trainer's credibility and well-being is not dependent on this person changing.

As the course draws to a close then the trainer will need to find effective ways of saying goodbye. What is effective will vary according to the people and the circumstances. Quite possibly deep relationships will have been established over a short period of time and saying goodbye will include appreciations, but also perhaps making statements of regret, e.g. 'I'm sorry that we never really got to know each other'. The trainer's main aim should be to 'finish his business' so that he does not carry his regrets, anger or sadness home to his family or over into the next course. Obviously this principle of finishing business also applies to the course members. Our experience is that the best way to say goodbye is *once*; long drawn-out goodbyes can be exhausting. Part of saying goodbye may well involve course feedback, whether formal or informal. We find it invaluable, as far as possible, to treat negative feedback purely as information to be considered and explored; equally we allow ourselves time to enjoy positive feedback.

Handling feelings

Despite having a general philosophy of finishing business the trainer may still come away from a training programme holding onto 'bad' feelings. This could have been the result of a conscious decision (e.g. 'It's not right for me to express my resentment towards that person; it wouldn't be appropriate in terms of the training design and objectives'); alternatively the unfinished business may 'pop-up' later, perhaps during reflection on the course. These feelings need to be dealt with.

One way could simply be for the trainer to decide to 'let go' of the feeling (i.e. decide not to feel that way any more). For others, some physical activity may be more satisfying and effective, perhaps playing squash or going for a long walk. Another way is to imagine that a pillow represents the person with whom the trainer is unfinished and then to shout or scream at it, possibly hitting it.

We have found these ways of releasing feelings important in clearing ourselves down prior to being able to think coolly and calmly about the training design and interventions and whether they were in any way the cause of what went wrong.

Getting support

As we mentioned earlier, interpersonal skills training is in many ways a helping profession and necessitates offering a lot of support. A consequence of this is that the trainer should have places and people where he can *receive* support. This requires recognising his own different needs and knowing where he can go to get these different needs met. For example, he may have a colleague who can offer him the support of intellectual discussion and challenge; his family may be able to offer him unconditional love; a training programme on which he is a course member may offer him the support of a safe environment in which to practise some new skills. Developing a support system requires a conscious strategy and may also include the establishment of contracts and trade-offs, e.g. the trainer may agree with his wife that when he gets home he will have half-an-hour of absolute peace and quiet, after which he will happily talk. Two colleagues might want to establish a contract about mutual counselling. These various sources of support can be valuable for reinforcing permissions (see p. 34).

Managing the workload

Working in the feeling area can be draining because of the demands it makes at the levels of both content and process. Effective programmes cannot be run if a sausage machine attitude is taken, i.e. assuming that it is a matter of cranking the handle and that courses can be produced like sausages. It is possible to argue that each course needs to be custom-built, with new activities and interventions being introduced depending on what is happening in the group.

Thus, the trainer's effectiveness cannot really be measured on the basis of the number of hours he teaches. The trainer therefore should do what he can to persuade others, such as his boss, that, for example, it may be counter-productive to fit in an additional course simply because a block of time has suddenly become available.

We have found as a rough guideline that our effectiveness substantially diminishes if we have more than twenty hours direct teaching contact with the group during a five-day course. Should the workload be particularly arduous during any period of time then we have found it necessary to put even greater reliance on the sorts of activities we have mentioned above e.g. support, physical fitness and attending personal growth groups.

CONCLUSION

It is fitting that the last chapter of this book should concern personal development since writing it has been a landmark in our own development. It has forced us to re-think and re-assess our values and ask fundamental questions such as, 'Why are we doing this type of work?'; 'What are we really trying to achieve?'; 'What right do we have to carry out personal process work?' Even as the chapters were being revised for the third or fourth time we found it necessary to change some of the basic emphases in order to incorporate some new learning and new experiences.

An interesting revelation for us has been how our different writing styles and approaches to writing have been a reflection of some differences we have in our styles and approach to interpersonal skills training. Seeing the words on the page (or not seeing them!) crystallised a number of personal issues of which we had been only dimly aware for some time. For us, therefore, this book has been a major achievement since it represents the successful resolution of these issues; we have been able to deal with an enormous amount of unfinished business.

We hope that our finished business will stimulate some unfinished business in the reader, namely a strong desire to learn more about and experience the excitement of personal process work.

LIST OF RESOURCES

There are a number of publications[1,2] which provide information on training resources and our aim is, as far as possible, to avoid duplication. We simply want to provide the reader with a start and what we offer here is in no way comprehensive. There is a brief description of the work of a variety of organisations, but we are not making specific recommendations. It is very much a matter of the reader getting further information and deciding who can best help him with his own particular needs.

Associates for Human Resources, Inc (A:HR)

A:HR provides a consultancy service, including organisational development work. Additionally, it has links with Beacon College in Boston by which it offers an MA Programme in humanistic psychology or Organisation Development. There is also a 'three month intensive' whose subject matter includes Gestalt, group dynamics and intervention strategies.

Contact:
Associates for Human Resources Inc.
191, Sudbury Road,
PO Box 727,
Concord
MA 01742
USA Tel: (617) 369–7810

Association for Humanistic Psychology (AHP)

This body links those who are interested in the 'growth movement' and, as with similar organisations, it encompasses with this philosophy many activities and training events, (e.g. Gestalt, group dynamics, spiritual awareness, Transactional Analysis).

Contact:
Association for Humanistic Psychology,
66, Southwark Bridge Road,
London,
SE1 OAS.
Tel: 01–928–8253
Copies of *Self and Society*, which is the European Journal of Humanistic Psychology, can be obtained from 66, Southwark Bridge Road.

Association of Teachers of Management (ATM)

The ATM is for those who are interested and/or involved in management development. It has a number of events and publications including a monthly newsletter, a journal (with articles and book reviews), special interest groups and annual workshops. At the workshops the offerings are usually diverse ranging from the 'technical'; e.g. corporate planning research methods, through to 'personal awareness'; e.g. biography work. These workshops are not run on a shopwindow basis but assume that the participant will stay with the particular workshop for the whole week.

Contact:
Marguerite Greatorex,
ATM
c/o Dept of Management Studies,
Polytechnic of Central London,
35, Marylebone Road,
London, NW1 5LS. (Tel: 01–486 5811 x 259)

British Association for Counselling (BAC)

The BAC has within it a number of specialist divisions for those who
are interested in particular applications of counselling, (e.g. counsell-
ing at work). It is also developing its own accreditation procedures.
The BAC Journal has articles as well as information on counselling
training.
Contact:
Celia Slinfield,
BAC,
37a, Sheep St,
Rugby, CV21 3BX. (Tel: 0788 78328/9)

The Gestalt Centre

This organisation offers an individualised training programme lasting
about four years. The key elements are on-going personal work, skill
development and assimilation of Gestalt theory. The training takes
place through weekly and weekend groups, seminars and residentials.
Peer support is encouraged and supervision is available for the
practising student. The training, except residentials, takes place at 7,
Parliament Hill, London NW5.
Contact:
Flora Hoskin,
17, The Dell,
St Albans,
Herts. (Tel: 0727 62297)

Group Relations Training Association (GRTA)

This is an educational charity which encompasses many aspects of the
'growth' movement. It is concerned to be 'open' to all those who
express an interest in its work and does not want to be, or become, a
professional body engaging, for example, in accreditation. Two of the
major events it offers are: Annual Group Relations Training Labora-

tory (i.e. 'T' Group); and its Annual Conference which provides a 'shopwindow' of different approaches for learning about oneself and others in the context of a group.
Contact:
Walter Truman Cox,
1, Gentian Close,
Birmingham, B31 1NN. (Tel: 021–475 4359)

Human Potential Resources

This is a directory containing information on a wide variety of events and training programmes related to personal awareness and development.
Contact:
Maureen Yeomans,
Human Potential Resources,
35, Station Road,
London, NW4 (Tel: 01–202 4941)

Institute of Transactional Analysis (ITA)

This organisation provides information on Transactional Analysis (TA) in the UK. It has recently developed its own accreditation procedures for professional membership. Its other facilities include a TA library, special interest networks (e.g. TA in Education) and an annual conference which attracts management trainers, therapists, social workers and others. The ITA News contains a list of TA groups in the UK.
Contact:
Institute of Transactional Analysis,
BM Box 4104.
London, WC1N 3XX. (Tel: 01–404 5011)

International Transactional Analysis Association (ITAA)

Until recently, this was the sole accrediting body for TA. Now others, such as the ITA and the European Association for Transactional Analysis, have developed their own qualifying procedures. Its quarterly journal has a variety of contents including elaboration of theory and descriptions of TA applications.
Contact:
International Transactional Analysis Association,
1772, Vallejo Street,

San Francisco,
California, 94123.
USA. (Tel: 415 885 5992)

National Organisation for Women's Management Education (NOWME)

This organisation is involved in the identification of women's training needs and is concerned to keep women informed about courses in management education.
Contact:
NOWME
29, Burkes Road,
Beaconsfield,
Bucks.

National Training Laboratories (NTL)

National Training Laboratories provides many opportunities for personal and professional development. It has specialist programmes for trainers and consultants, including a Trainer Apprenticeship Programme through which the participant can act as a co-trainer and receive comprehensive assessments.
Contact:
NTL Institute,
PO Box 9155,
Rosslyn Station,
Arlington,
VA 22209,
USA. Tel: (703) 527–1500

The Omega Institute for Holistic Studies

As its title suggests, this organisation is concerned with the 'whole person' and offers many different types of training events to increase self-awareness.
Contact:
The Omega Institute,
Lake Drive,
R D 2,
Box 377,
Rhinebeck, NY 12572.
USA. Tel: (914) 266 4301 *or* (914) 876 2058

The Open Centre

This centre offers a range of groups with different orientations to learning about oneself. There are opportunities to learn through Gestalt and Transactional Analysis; additionally, other approaches are covered including meditation and body awareness.
Contact:
The Open Centre,
188, Old Street,
London, EC1. Tel: 01–278 6783

Organisation Development Network

This organisation provides a link for those who are interested in, and want to discuss with others, ways of making organisations more effective. Its membership is varied including trainers, personnel specialists, operational researchers, economists etc. There is an annual conference and a monthly newsletter; regional groups meet in London, the South West, the North West, Scotland and the Midlands.
Contact:
Patricia Coleman-Smith,
Latchetts,
Butchers Lane,
Preston,
Hitchin, Herts.
SG4 7TR (Tel: 0462 59563)

The Tavistock Institute of Human Relations

The Tavistock Institute of Human Relations offers a variety of services including consultancy and general courses. The courses usually have a strong 'here and now' focus and are intended to give the participants an opportunity to explore such key issues as authority, leadership boundaries and the 'unconscious processes' which can dramatically affect the effectiveness of groups.
Contact:
The Tavistock Institute of Human Relations,
The Tavistock Centre,
Belsize Lane,
London, NW3 5BA. (Tel: 01–435 7111 x 383)

or A K Rice Institute,
1610, New Hampshire Ave NW

Washington, DC 20009
USA.

University Associates International

This organisation provides a wealth of material for the interpersonal skills trainer. Two of their major publications are: *Structured Experiences*, a series published annually which contains exercises together with details on handling and *Annual Handbook*, a series of books which have not only exercises but short outlines of theory and lists of resources.
Contact:
University Associates International,
Challenge House,
45/47, Victoria Street,
Mansfield,
Nottingham. NG18 5SU (Tel: 0623 640203)

or University Associates Inc,
8517 Production Ave,
P O Box 26240,
San Diego
California, 92126
USA (Tel: 619 578 5900)

Women and Training News (Sponsored by the MSC)

(The Co-ordinating Group for the Development of Training for Women) Its aims are similar to NOWME (see p. 125). It is also involved in developing a network and platform for women to express issues (ethical, professional and personal) that are affecting career development. It also gives information on current courses, publications, conferences and events.
Contact:
Ann Cooke
Group Co-ordinator
c/o Department of Managerial Studies, Gloucester College of Arts and Technology,
Oxstalls Lane,
Gloucester, GL2 9HW. (0452 501795)

Bookshops

Compendium Bookshop,
234, Camden High Street,
London, NW1. (01–485 8944)

Dillon's University Bookshop,
1, Malet Street,
London, WC1E 7JB

Prometheus,
134, Alcester Road,
Moseley,
Birmingham, B13 8EE

National Marriage Guidance Council Bookshop,
Herbert Gray College,
Little Church Street,
Rugby,
Warks. CV21 3AP. (0788 73241)

'Changes' Bookshop,
242, Belsize Road,
London, NW6. (01-328 5161)

Journals (some selected examples)

Journal of European Industrial Training,
MCB Publications Ltd,
198/200 Keighley Road,
Bradford,
W. Yorks. BD9 4JQ
It is published quarterly and includes articles and book reviews.

Human Potential Resources (see p. 124)

Self and Society (See p. 122)

Journal of the British Association for Counselling (See p. 123)

Management Education and Development (Journal of the Association of Teachers of Management) (See p. 123)

ITA News, published by the Institute for Transactional Analysis (See p. 124)

Transactional Analysis Journal and *Script* both published by the International Transactional Analysis Association (See p. 124)

References

1 'Personnel and Training Datebook,' published annually by Kogan Page
2 Phillips K. and Fraser T. *The Management of Interpersonal Skills Training* Gower, 1982

APPENDIX A
TRANSACTIONAL ANALYSIS (TA) IN PERSONAL PROCESS WORK

The aims of this appendix are to provide a brief summary of TA theory and to examine how it can be used in personal process work. Our intention is not to cover all aspects of theory, but sufficient to give the reader a basic understanding of some essential points. With this information the reader should then be able to decide whether to go further in learning about and applying TA.

TA THEORY

Eric Berne (1910–70), the originator of TA, was a psychiatrist whose chief concerns included a desire to 'cure' people as quickly as possible. As a result he tended to move away from his psychoanalytic background and sought to develop a means for quick diagnosis, making tightly focused interventions essentially at the behavioural level. In other words, he became less interested in the traditional psychoanalytic approach of analysing and interpreting the history and detail of his client's internal processes.

Two skills which he drew on in developing his new philosophy were intuition, and attention to behavioural detail. The latter skill led him, in time, to identify certain clusters of behaviour, and to be able, through intuition, to guess quite accurately what thoughts and feelings lay behind them. These clusters of behaviour Berne termed 'ego states', and he suggested that there were three.

Parent ego state

Those patterns of behaviour which people particularly acquire from 'significant' authority figures in childhood; for most these would be their parents. However, even when fully grown up one can acquire new Parent values, e.g. through the influence of a particular boss.

There are two facets to the Parent ego state: Critical Parent (CP) whose typical behaviours include, 'You must . . ', 'You ought to . . . '; values and beliefs are stated in a strong, often judgemental way. The Nurturing Parent (NP) is usually supportive, sometimes smothering and is often concerned to take care of others e.g. 'Don't worry I'll sort it out for you . . . '

Adult ego state (A)

This pattern of behaviour is characterised by detachment, and thinking in a clear, possibly overly clinical way about problems. It is essentially an information seeker, giver and receiver. Consequently the frequent use, in a calm way, of such words as 'Who?', 'Why?', 'How?'

Child ego state

This is concerned with feelings and behaviours, many of which have been acquired in childhood and continue to have an impact in the present. One facet of the Child ego state, the Free Child (FC), can be curious, fun loving, egocentric and selfish. The newly-born child epitomises the Free Child ego state. The other facet, the Adapted Child (AC), is that part of people which was modified in order to get along with and/or get attention from authority figures in the past (e.g. 'I know Mummy will be pleased with me if I eat my greens').

The Child Ego state is generally regarded as having another aspect, the Little Professor (LP). This is a significant source of intuition and creativity. However, many believe that a specific set of behaviours cannot be attributed to it, and that it acts as an internal trigger for other ego states – hence it is not shown in Table A1. This table gives more detail on the various aspects of the ego states.

The standard way of diagramming the ego states is shown in Figure A1. All the ego states can function in a positive or negative way as is shown by Table A2.

It has already been stated that Berne was concerned to effect a quick cure. In many ways this meant for him paying attention to how people used their ego states to *transact* with one another, and also to consider

Table A1
Attributes of the ego states

Ego state	Typical words/phrases	Typical voice tones	Typical behaviours	Typical attitudes
Critical Parent	That's disgraceful You ought You must always Don't ask questions Because I said so Ridiculous	Sneering Angry Condescending Critical/stern Disgusted Emphatic	Furrowed brow Pointed finger Scowling face Set jaw Pounding on table Crossed arms	Moralistic Judgemental Authoritarian Opinionated Protective
Nurturing Parent	Well done, young man What a splendid effort Don't worry I'll sort it out for you	Sympathetic Encouraging Comforting Loving	Pat on back Consoling touch Benevolent smile Offering support	Caring Supportive Understanding Smothering Looking for waifs and strays
Adult	How? When? Where? Let's look at it again It's 6.30 What are the options?	Clear Calm Enquiring Without strong emotion	Relaxed Attentive and aware Level eye contact Note taking	Non-judgemental Open-minded Interested Confident Attentive Clinical

Ego state	Typical words/phrases	Typical voice tones	Typical behaviours	Typical attitudes
Little professor (Often a trigger for other ego state behaviours)	My hunch is . . . I've got a feeling that . . . Where do babies come from?	Sneaky Inquisitive	Manipulative Winking Intuitive Creative	Superstitious 'Survival' thinking e.g. What do I have to do to get appreciation?
Adapted Child	I'll try hard Please can I? Sorry I can't Please Thank you	Whiny Placating Mumbling Taunting Argumentative	Polite Downcast eyes Vigorous head-nodding Nail biting Slumped and dejected posture Spitefulness Confused	Compliant Defiant Delaying Passive Complaining Respectful
Free Child	I want Wow! I feel great!	Loud Fast Playful Excited	Laughing with someone Demonstration of feelings Self-centred Impulsive	Curious Energetic Fun loving Spontaneous

Figure A1 The ego states

Table A2
Positive and negative aspects of ego states*

	Positive	Negative
CP	Warning of danger – Don't touch that electric fire! Disciplinary – I'm not prepared to put up with this sort of behaviour for much longer.	Dominating and constricting – You're stupid, You never get anything right!
NP	Caring and supportive – Don't worry, I'll support you in any decision you make	Smothering – Don't worry, I'll sort it all out for you.
A	Problem-solving – What are the alternatives? What exactly happened?	Cold and distant – I understand that you are upset about your wife leaving you. It would appear that there are three courses of action open to you . . .
AC	Polite/courteous – I'm sorry. Please may I . . . ?	Over-compliant. Sycophantic. Rebellious in order to gain attention.
FC	Loving, sexy, warm, open, intimate, close.	Egocentric. Selfish

what might be the most effective types of transactions he could make as a therapist.

This approach appeared to be particularly valuable where a person was not using a full range of ego states, and their various facets, but was stuck using just one or two, e.g. compulsively using the Critical

*Reprinted from *The Management of Interpersonal Skills Training* by Keri Phillips and T. Fraser (Gower, 1982)

Parent to relate to others, when it might have been much more productive to use Adapted Child or Nurturing Parent. Berne, therefore, was interested in the ways in which destructive patterns of behaviour might be broken using different types of transactions.

This approach has strong parallels with the handling of difficult relationships at work and is the basis of the application of TA to organisations.[1] For example a subordinate might spend much of his time in his Adapted Child and want to 'hook' the Nurturing Parent in his boss so that he does not have to take any responsibility for making decisions; i.e. he avoids using his own Parent or Adult ego states.

If he succeeds then the general pattern of his transactions could well be as shown in Figure A2.

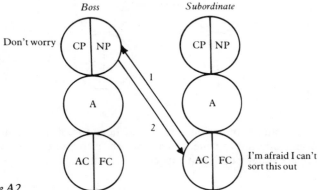

Figure A2

If the boss were aware of this then he might cross the transaction, as shown in Figure A3.

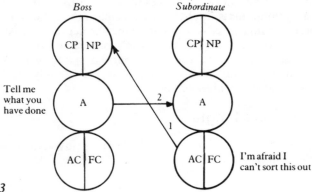

Figure A3

Figure A3 shows an 'invitation' by the boss to the subordinate to relate to him in a different way. In the other instance the boss might use two ego states at the same time, perhaps using Adult words but backing it up with some Nurturing Parent non-verbal behaviour in terms of smiles and nods, as shown in Figure A4.

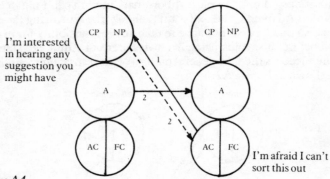

I'm interested in hearing any suggestion you might have

I'm afraid I can't sort this out

Figure A4

Ego states and transactions are the cornerstone of TA, hence the considerable amount of time we have spent on them here. Nevertheless there are other important aspects to TA theory:

Strokes

These are 'units of recognition' and may be 'positive' or 'negative'. The subordinate in the previous example may focus on the negative in himself (e.g. 'I'm stupid; I can never get anything right'), and, as a result 'encourage' negative strokes from others by saying, e.g. 'You'll probably think this is stupid but . . . '. One of the options the boss has in these circumstances is to avoid giving the negative stroke (i.e. not say, 'yes you are right it is stupid') but rather to look out for opportunities to stroke the behaviour he wants, e.g. When the subordinate uses his initiative then to say, 'I'm really glad that you came up with some ideas of your own'.

The drama triangle[2]

It is possible to analyse many social situations (involving two or more people) in terms of the 'drama triangle'(See Figure A5)

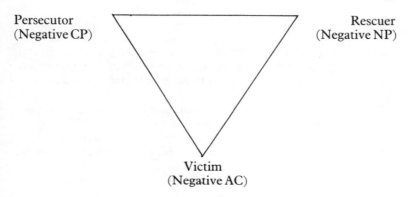

Figure A5

According to the drama triangle, individuals can quickly fall into one of three roles – persecutor, rescuer, or victim. (Each of these roles reflects the negative aspects of a certain ego state – namely Critical Parent, Nurturing Parent and Adapted Child). In the playing out of any one situation the individuals can quickly switch the roles between themselves, e.g. a trainer (persecutor) is reviewing a course member's role-play by pointing out every conceivable 'mistake'. The co-trainer (rescuer) tries to intervene to protect the course member, who then joins with the rest of the group (in a persecutor role) to attack both the trainers who end up feeling inadequate (i.e. victim position).

The persecutor works from an assumption that he is better than others (i.e. a Life Position of I+U– see p. 138) and consequently looks for the weaknesses in others, and generally wants to put others down either verbally or physically.

The rescuer keeps offering help even when it is not needed and sees his role in life as looking after others. An assumption is made that others are inadequate and cannot solve their own problems (i.e. Life Position of I+U–).

The victim takes a one down position (I–U+) and 'hooks' rescuers into offering help or persecutors into finding fault. This person accentuates his own weaknesses.

These roles are mutually dependent and a pattern of transactions and relationships is set up whereby each person's way of looking at the world is destructively reinforced.

Games

These are short series of transactions in which the game players end up reinforcing a negative perception of themselves and/or each other. Games may be played from any of the drama triangle positions.

Persecutor

Nigysob (Now I've got you, you son of a bitch. The person who typically tries to put others down).

Blemish (The person who always finds something wrong)

Let's you and him fight (The person who sets up arguments among others)

Rescuer

I'm only trying to help you (The person who keeps offering help – even when it is not needed – and is often upset when it is rejected)

What would you do without me? (The person who likes to think he is indispensable)

Victim

Kick me (The person who contrives to put himself down)

Why does this always happen to me? (The person who feels that he is always losing out)

Stupid (The person who 'pretends' that he is too stupid to understand anything)

Do me something (The person who always expects others to solve his problems)

Scripts[3]

This idea integrates a number of TA theories and explores how in early life children can make unconscious decisions about who they are, the type of life they are going to live and what the world is like. This leads to certain ego states being over-used, particular types of games being played and a pattern of 'stroking'. Life then becomes a self-fulfilling prophesy. For example the boy who grows up believing that it is his role in life to look after people and seeks, outside his awareness, jobs where he can do this. He becomes a boss and attracts to him subordinates whose script involves their taking a one-down position and finding somebody to look after them.

Life Positions[4]

An essential determinant of people's script decisions is their 'life position'. TA theory is based on the assumption that, at an early age, each child makes a decision about whether he/she is better than, worse than or equal to, everybody else. There are four basic life positions which reflect these decisions, as shown in Table A2.

Table A2

I'm not OK, You're OK (*I−U+*)	*I'm OK, You're OK (I+U+)*
Strong in negative aspects of Adapted Child	Positive aspects of all ego states.
Victim	Not on the Drama Triangle
Gives self a lot of negative strokes	Gives a wide range of positive and negative strokes, *as appropriate*.
Some typical feelings are: guilt, hurt, ashamed, stupid.	Some typical feelings are: contentment, appropriate anger, trusting
I'm not OK, You're not OK (*I−U−*)	*I'm OK, You're not OK* (*I+U−*)
Strong in negative aspects of Adapted Child	Strong in negative aspects of Nurturing and Critical Parent.
Victim	Rescuer/Persecutor
Gives self and others a lot of negative strokes.	Gives other a lot of negative and/or phoney positive strokes.
Some typical feelings are: despair, apathy, weak, rejected.	Some typical feelings are: self-righteousness, indignation, hostility.

Two key points about life positions are firstly that they reflect general orientations to life. It is unlikely that anybody could spend all their time, for example, in I+U+. Certain events could happen during the course of a day in which the person might slip into the other positions. However, their general approach to life and relationships is likely to be reflected in just one of the life positions.

The second point in fact relates to TA generally. TA is based on the assumption that people can change. So, somebody who realises that his general life position is I−U+ can make conscious decisions about his stroking patterns, ego states etc. in order to achieve more productive and satisfying relationships, and thus to lead a more fulfilling life.

TA IN PERSONAL PROCESS WORK

TA is sufficiently versatile to make a contribution in many aspects of interpersonal skills training. However our main concern here is to make some points on its use in unstructured, feeling-based programmes.

General points

1   When using TA in personal process work it is essential that the trainer has a good understanding of himself in TA terms, so that he is aware, for example, of his stroking patterns, of the drama triangle position he finds it easiest to slip into, the types of games by which he can 'hook' himself or others.
2   TA can be used explicitly or implicitly for making process interventions. If it is used explicitly then TA words and concepts will be used openly; e.g. 'What does your Adult say about . . . ?' If it is used implicitly then TA words are not used but TA values are; e.g. 'Ask for some appreciations from the group'. This is to encourage someone who has a tendency to get into the victim position to ask for positive strokes.
3   TA can be used in conjunction with other approaches e.g. Gestalt, Psychodrama and Encounter.
4   TA can be used for work between the trainer and one trainee or with a high degree of group involvement (see below).
5   As is also shown below, TA can be used for making 'higher' or 'lower' risk interventions. However, as we have said before a trainee's sense of risk is clearly subjective and what is high risk for one person can be experienced by another as low risk.

TA-based interventions and activities

The description of interventions and activities which follows does not have a particular sequence and we rely on the reader to follow his interest, selecting out and adapting the material so that it fits in with his own values, approach and aims.

'My interpretation of what you're saying is . . . ', possibly accompanied by drawing on the board. This is probably a lower risk intervention because it is an invitation to the trainee to think and analyse rather than do. The main danger is that he may swallow it whole using his Adapted Child rather than Adult – 'Oh, so that's how I am'. Part of the seductive quality of TA is that it can appear to give the complete answer, whereas it is simply *a* perspective. Sometimes people use TA to avoid responsibility in their relationships; 'It's not me it's my Adapted Child'.

'What is your TA interpretation of what you have been describing?'. This is an invitation to the trainee to think, using his Adult. It can also lead to group discussion and feedback, as well as giving the trainer a breathing space. It can also be valuable as a way of checking conceptual understanding as well as increasing personal awareness. There is, however, a danger of an excess of labelling and searching for *the* definitive analysis rather than something which will be of immediate practical help to the trainee.

Chair work (examples):
– An illustration, and the working through, of an internal dialogue with the chairs representing various ego states. For example, in relating to his boss a manager may be stuck in an impasse where his Parent energy wants to tell him (i.e. the boss) off and his Child energy is invested in being scared. Sometimes an Adult chair is important for helping the trainee to think about and identify options. However, the Adult chair can end up being unhelpful for those who already find it easy to 'think' and thus block themselves from expressing their feelings. The trainer may well be faced in this approach with decisions about how far he works at the level of behavioural options and how far he works at the level of internal processes and feelings.
– Using the chairs, representing various ego states, to relate to other group members, e.g. using the Nurturing Parent chair to express some caring to a course colleague. This may well be higher risk because of its focus on 'here and now' relationships. A balance to this is that the group may be a powerful source of direct and indirect support.
   (Where the chairs are used to relive an event from the distant past (e.g. early childhood experience) this venture into the 'there and then' is a high risk of intervention probably inappropriate for a management course.)

'What ego state are you in now?' This can be a higher risk intervention because of its focus on the here and now. The group may be invited to offer their feedback as well, although there is then a possibility of the recipient being overwhelmed or pressurised. The chances of this happening are reduced if the trainer allows just one item of feedback at a time and checks the recipient's feelings about the giver of the feedback.

'How can you use your Critical Parent constructively in this group?' This encourages the trainee not necessarily to switch ego states but to build on what he already does in a more constructive way, (i.e. switching from –CP to +CP). This can be a big permission since the trainee is being told, 'You are OK as you are, you don't need to make any dramatic changes'. It is a way of 'stroking the resistance',[5] and implicitly saying, 'You do not have to be different'. The cycle of pressure and resistance referred to elsewhere is then less likely to happen.

'Practise using your Nurturing Parent in the group'. This is an example of guiding the trainee to experiment in using an ego state which he finds uncomfortable and/or rarely uses. Any sort of experimentation will require support from the trainer and the group (i.e. positive strokes, but not rescuing). It may help to switch to looking at the internal process if the trainee finds it difficult to start ('What's happening?'; 'How are you stopping yourself?'; 'What are you feeling?').

'Use different ego states to give me some feedback?'. This can be helpful if the trainer believes/feels that there is some uncertainty about him or his role. It may be important for the co-trainer, if there is one, to be present so that he can act as an intermediary or process consultant – but without getting on the drama triangle!

'How might you blame yourself for what you have just done?' 'How long are you going to blame yourself?' A move to pre-empt somebody with a strong internal negative CP; i.e. they find it easy to blame themselves and give themselves negative strokes. Any change involves some risk and it is our assumption that the risk is particularly high for those who have a strong internal negative Critical Parent which could severely punish them for breaking an old rule. A follow-up intervention might be, 'What are you going to do rather than blame yourself?'.

'How might you sabotage yourself?'. A move to pre-empt somebody's rebellious, self-destructive Child which can block change. An Adult to Adult contract will not 'stick' if there is an unhappy or unconvinced Child in the background looking for a 'let-out'. Our experience is that people are normally very clear on how they might sabotage a particular commitment to change.

'What rules do you have about relationships at work?' (or 'here'). Encouraging the trainee to explore his/her Parent and re-assess through Adult awareness, and possible experimentation, their current validity. In any experimentation the trainee should be given and get for himself plenty of support because he may 'rubberband'[6] into the past and feel like a five-year-old telling his father off. One way of reducing the chances of 'rubberbanding' is to keep the trainee focused outwards (e.g. on what he sees) rather than inwards (e.g. on what he feels).

Arrange the group around the room according to your estimate of their favourite ego states/drama triangle positions. This can be a way of bringing alive and to the surface process issues within the group. There are many options which can follow on from this: exploring feelings; practice in getting into different ego states/ drama triangle positions; one individual explaining to another individual the pay-off he gets from adopting a 'favourite' role. Often the simple act of getting up and moving around generates energy which can then be used to explore, experiment with, and possibly break old patterns.

Paper and pencil exercises with small and/or large group review. These can be used to introduce quite a wide variety of risk levels. The paper and pencil aspect is to encourage Adult analysis and the small group review probably retains the element of safety. It may then be that the sense of safety is sufficiently strong to allow extensive consideration and discussion in the full group. An example of this general approach is given in pp. 142–3.

'Exaggerate that 'small feeling of irritation' and express it towards the person concerned'. This is to focus on Adapted Child minimisation. It could end up being higher risk with a discharge, catharsis, of years of bottled up feelings.

'I've got a hunch that . . . ' This can be a particularly powerful way of giving permission to use intuition; a useful counter-balance to those groups whose background is strongly influenced by a strong belief in absolute right answers.

Additional general points about TA in personal process work

The group is an important resource for the trainer and each trainee, e.g. giving feedback, as 'material' for experiments, allowing the trainer some thinking time so that he can check his own boundaries, and interventions.

Any experiments, whether during or after the course, are likely to be more productive if they are at the level of a 'small step at a time', and with which the trainee is comfortable in terms of his own Parent, Adult and Child (i.e. it accords with his moral values, makes sense and feels right). The bigger the step, the bigger the risk and the greater are the chances of internal sabotage (see above) or external sabotage (i.e. others pressurising him to go back to his 'old ways'.)

The trainer can use his ego states constructively by:

+ CP = Protection,[7] setting limits, managing and controlling the pattern of events so that the trainee does not physically or emotionally do harm to himself or others. 'I really think you ought to . . . '; 'You must . . . '; 'Make sure that . . . '.

+ NP = Permission,[7] 'It's OK to try something different, to experiment and take risks.' Giving positive strokes, verbally and non-verbally.

+ A = Thinking, analysing, enquiring, challenging, encouraging the trainee to identify options. The trainer can and should use his Adult to be aware of himself and the patterns, constructive and destructive, of his Parent and Child ego states.

+ FC = Potency[7] through authenticity and sharing feelings. Using the FC to be a clear and visible presence and to have fun.

+ LP = Using intuition and hunches; to be sensitive to unspoken/process communications, to fill in creatively the gaps in what the trainee is concerned about and then to use Adult to check on assumptions.

CONCLUSION

TA has a significant contribution to make in the interpersonal skills training of managers and trainers. It can be used implicitly where the trainer or manager keeps the model in his head and uses it to analyse and break the unproductive patterns he and others get into. Equally TA can be used explicitly for an open sharing of ideas and feelings and carrying out personal process work.

References

1   Barker D.M. *T.A. and Training – the theory and use of Transactional Analysis in organisations*, Gower 1982.
2   This idea was developed by Steve Karpman see 'Fairy tales and script drama analysis. *Transactional Analysis Bulletin* Vol. 7 No. 26. 1968.
3   For an excellent book on scripts see Steiner C. *Scripts People Live*, Grove Press, 1974.
4   This idea was developed by Franklyn Ernst, see 'The OK corral:

the grid for get-on-with' *Transactional Analysis Journal*, Vol. 1
   No. 4. 1974.
5 The idea of 'stroking the resistance' was we believe, developed by
   Kristy Huige.
6 Barnes G. (ed) *T.A. After Eric Berne* Harpers College Press, 1977
   p. 346.
7 Crossman P. 'Permission and Protection' *TA Bulletin* Vol . 5 No.
   19 (1963) pp. 152–3, (also Klein M. *'Lives People Live'* Wiley 1980
   pp 125–6)

APPENDIX B
GESTALT IN PERSONAL PROCESS WORK

The aims of this appendix are to provide a brief summary of Gestalt theory and to examine how it can be used in personal process work.

GESTALT THEORY

The word 'gestalt' is German and is difficult to translate precisely into English. Roughly it means 'form', 'pattern' or 'configuration', and refers to the process of integrating a series of detailed perceptions into a complete experience or meaningful image which is more than the sum of its parts. For example, someone listening to a piece of music does not hear a series of individual notes but a melody.

This process of forming a gestalt was first discovered in the latter part of the nineteenth century by a group of German psychologists who observed human and animal behaviour in order to understand how man's perceptions of his environment influence his learning. Another important characteristic of perception, they discovered, is the individual's movement toward closure. A figure is seen as a complete bounded image – in some cases the perceiver even visually compenstates for gaps in outline as, for example, in seeing these separate dots as a complete circle.

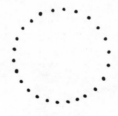

The psychologists also discovered that any incomplete gestalt represents an 'unfinished situation' that clamours for attention and interferes with the formation of any new gestalt. A simple example of this process is the person who, some few hours before a dental appointment, has difficulty in concentrating on any activity for a reasonable length of time. The emerging gestalt of the dental appointment blocks out all other 'gestalten' and he fails to deal satisfactorily with any other task.[1]

Frederick ('Fritz') S. Perls (1893–1970), now recognised as the founder of Gestalt therapy, began to apply these ideas in the field of psychotherapy in the 1940s. Perls originally qualified as a doctor in Berlin in 1921. He was trained in psychoanalysis at the Psychoanalytic Institutes of Berlin, Frankfurt and Vienna. Although he later described himself as 'not a pure Gestaltist'[2] Perls was particularly interested in the idea of the unfinished situation, the incomplete gestalt.

Gestalt formation and destruction

The central concept of the Gestalt approach is that personal needs arise and are satisfied in a pattern of gestalt formations and destructions. For example; it is late evening and a man is sitting comfortably in an armchair reading an absorbing book in a centrally-heated home. Although he is not aware of it, the heating system switches off automatically and the room begins to cool. At this stage the book continues to hold his attention and forms the foreground or 'figure'; the cooling temperature is the background, or 'ground'. At first he is not aware of the drop in temperature, but gradually, as it becomes colder, he begins to respond to the change unconsciously. He tucks his legs beneath him and moves slightly in order to sit more compactly and retain body heat. His conscious attention, however, is still entirely in the book whilst his body begins to respond to another need. The gestalt, in relation to his need for warmth, is beginning to form, although it has not yet become 'figure'.

Gradually, as the temperature drops, his discomfort penetrates increasingly into his awareness. He makes additional efforts to ignore the cold and maintain his involvement with the book but there comes a point at which he can no longer sustain his interest in reading. At this point the existing need or interest is destroyed in favour of a new one – the need to maintain body comfort through warmth. The new gestalt emerges into and now occupies the centre of his attention. He leaves the book and the chair and takes some action designed to restore his comfort – he turns the heating back on.

Once he is warm again he can pick up the book and quickly the temperature, along with other possible concerns, becomes part of the ground, and the book's contents begin to absorb him again.

Needs are present in a hierarchy so priorities resulting from the relationship between the individual and the environment are fulfilled, drop away and are replaced by other needs. The cycle of Gestalt formation and destruction is diagrammatically shown in Figure B1.

Relating this model to the episode of the central heating it can be seen that the 'new situation' was prompted by a drop in room temperature. The 'need' for maintaining body warmth was signalled by 'awareness' of physical discomfort. The 'action' of turning the central heating on involved 'contact' with the switch and this led to 'satisfaction' of the need.

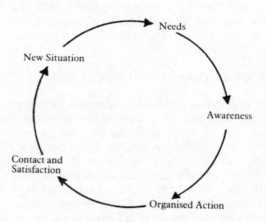

Figure B1 Gestalt formation and destruction

All those but the mentally or physically sick and the poor or oppressed can orient and organise themselves sufficiently to satisfy their needs concerned with most physical functions. The majority find breathing, eating, drinking, excreting and resting, fairly straightforward and satisfying, although this is not as obvious as it perhaps seems at first glance. People who eat too much, drink too much, suffer from constipation or insomnia are often not thought of as ill, but for these people even fundamental physical functioning, let alone the more complex emotional and psychological needs, presents difficulties.

The emotional and psychological needs are more elusive. For example, the need to give and receive approval, love, recognition, companionship, stimulation, interest, acceptance and communication. In these circumstances the individual may have problems in perceiving his need clearly or may not know how to satisfy the need. When dealing with one or all of these needs his experience may be a sense of uneasiness or confusion.

An example in management might be an employee's uneasy feeling that his boss treats other members of his group of subordinates in a more relaxed, informal way. He may seem to talk with them frequently, freely and with warmth. But with this employee the boss is rather formal and more abrupt. The employee perhaps feels hurt and isolated and finds himself pulling back from contact both with the boss and his peers. This dissatisfaction leads to a sense of isolation, low motivation and a drop in work output which in itself produces a vicious circle. The employee tells himself there is nothing he can do: either he carries on as he is or he goes and finds another job.

Here the need for personal recognition and acceptance remains unsatisfied and being 'unfinished business' disturbs the healthy pattern of emerging needs and their satisfaction. In this way collections of unfinished business impede the individual so that his vision becomes less clear and he becomes less ready for the next experience.

Interruptions

The Gestalt approach is directly concerned with the ways in which the individual can interrupt the cycle of need satisfaction. These interruptions are learned patterns of behaviour which made sense at some stage in his life – usually in the relationship with his parents – but now are often inappropriate in relationships with others. There are five types of interruption:

1   *Introjection* – involves accepting a set of rules and standards either because someone has told the person to do so, and reinforced their statement by punishment and/or reward, or because they are fashionable or safe or traditional, or dangerous or revolutionary. These undigested attitudes, ways of acting, feeling and evaluating are called introjects, e.g. men should never cry.

2   *Projection* – involves seeing in others qualities, attitudes, behaviours, which the individual disowns in himself, e.g. the arrogant man who denies the quality in himself but experiences himself as being surrounded by arrogant people.

3   *Retroflection* – involves the individual turning back upon himself feelings that are really directed at people around him, e.g. instead of expressing his anger at another the retroflector turns it in upon himself and ends up feeling guilty.

4   *Confluence* – involves the individual operating from a kind of emotional colour-blindness, i.e. he sees his own needs as unimportant, he is out of touch with his feelings, and he does not discriminate in his relationships with others.

5   *Egotism* – involves the individual stepping outside his self and from a distance offering a commentary on the self, others, and the relationship between the two, e.g. talking about his concern for another instead of expressing that concern through physical contact.

Although it is possible to distinguish between and to describe the five different types of interruption, it is important to say that they rarely occur in isolation. An individual is likely to compound the process of interrupting the cycle of need fulfilment, for example, with combinations of introjects ('I must not show my feelings'), retroflection (clenching the jaw to hold back anger) and confluence (failing to notice his own actions).

GESTALT IN PERSONAL PROCESS WORK

In the last ten years Gestalt has been used in both the areas of interpersonal skills training and in organisation development (see Herman and Korenich[3]). Although Gestalt can be used on structured doing/feeling-based programmes, the approach is more effectively suited to unstructured feeling-based training (see Chapter 4). On such programmes the trainer will introduce ground rules to facilitate learning. This he may do either explicitly at the start of a group, or gradually over a period of time. These ground rules are intended to set the appropriate conditions for personal experimentation by confronting many of the socially and organisationally accepted patterns for interpersonal behaviour. They are not intended as 'musts' or 'shoulds'. Following the ground rules in a mechanical way, or dutifully playing 'good trainee', is a negation of the Gestalt approach.

Ground Rules

'Here and Now' Experience

In common with other approaches to interpersonal skills training, course members are asked to pay attention to their own feelings, sensations and behaviours as they occur. The purpose of this rule is to develop awareness, since it is awareness which provides the raw material for self-development. Paying attention to events such as breathing, tensions, self-stroking, avoiding contact, excitement, interest, memories, images, irritation and rejection provides the individual with valuable information about who he is and what he wants at the moment. Talking about the past or future results in little contact with others, and limits the possibility of increasing self-awareness.

Personal responsibility

Every thought, feeling, statement and action is an expression of the person's identity at the moment. So course members are asked to 'own' or identify with what they are saying or doing. Many people have learnt to say 'one', 'we', 'people' or 'you' when they really mean 'I', and 'can't' when they mean 'won't'. The response 'You can't go round saying that sort of thing', is a typical example. The clearer statement would be 'I won't say that'. The 'you' is changed to 'I' since the individual is actually talking about the prospect of his own actions, and the 'can't' is changed to 'won't' since the suggestion (for example, telling each member of the group something about them which he finds attractive) clearly is feasible and the issue is the person's willingness rather than ability. This groundrule serves to highlight confluence and projections in substituting 'I' for 'we' or 'people'. Each individual is encouraged to speak for himself, or at least to check with each member of the group about their experience to see if he is saying something that others agree with.

Questions

'Why' questions are generally discouraged for they invite individuals to 'talk about' instead of making contact and learning. In responding to such a question, e.g. 'Why are you silent?', an individual is capable of producing any number of plausible reasons, e.g. 'I'm always silent in groups'; 'I have nothing to say' etc, and be no nearer to understanding who he is. For each of these responses begets another question, e.g. 'Why are you always silent in groups?'; and so on and so on. By following such questions the individual ends up in the labyrinth of introspection. Often the 'why' question is an invitation for a person to explain, defend, or justify some aspect of himself or his existence. For example, 'Why did you say that to Alan?' may conceal the statement 'I do not like what you said'. For this reason the trainer may invite a questioner to check whether there is a statement behind his question. Developing awareness involves exploring the 'whats' and 'hows' of behaviour. So Gestalt trainers will make frequent interventions in the group by asking questions like 'What are you doing now?' to someone who has stopped speaking, for instance) and 'How do you make yourself angry/scared/sad etc?'

Being Specific

When speaking to each other, course members are encouraged to be direct, using the words 'I' and 'you' in their statements, e.g. 'I don't trust you'. Only in this way can they begin to explore and make contact with each other. In addition to taking responsibility for his actions the course member is identifying directly with those parts of himself he may be projecting onto others. In the example above the speaker may be saying more about his lack of trust in himself than about the recipient of the feedback. Similarly, the simple expedient of changing all 'it' statements into specific terms enables the individual to develop increased awareness of his own experiences. To say, 'I feel cold now', instead of, 'It is cold now', brings him closer to his experience. The use of the word 'it' applied to self and others is one way to keep distant from the experience.

Simple Statements

Course members are asked to describe their experiences in the simplest terms; 'I feel lonely', 'My head aches'; 'I am confused'. Feelings and sensations are essentially simple experiences. Elaborate statements are often distorted with explanations or avoidance. For example, the statement 'I sort of feel unhappy . . . sometimes . . . it is most unusual'; may well mean, 'I feel sad'.

Interpretation

Interpreting behaviour can be more of a hindrance than a help. When a person makes a statement about how he responds to the behaviour of another that is self-expression. When he interprets the meaning of another's behaviour that statement implies that the speaker knows what is motivating the other – which is fantasy. Most interpretations are based on projections – even if they are confirmed to be correct by the person on the receiving end – and say as much about the speaker as the receiver. The person who says to another course member, 'I guess you had a tough time as a child', is likely to be asked by the trainer if that is also a statement about himself. The usual practice in Gestalt groups is to clearly prefix an interpretation with the words, 'I guess that . . . ' or 'I imagine that . . . '

It is because of the strong discouragement of 'intellectualising' (e.g.

interpreting, understanding, conceptualising etc.) that Gestalt is invariably used for making process interventions without any reference to the theory or concepts, e.g. 'How are you stopping yourself from asking for appreciations?' At the end of a piece of work the trainer may offer as feedback some interpretation of the process, e.g. 'I saw you denying your own anger by believing that it was Bill who was angry with you'. But, primarily, the trainer will be intervening to help the individual to become aware of his behaviour from moment to moment. To this end he will use three basic interventions:

What are you doing?
What are you feeling?
What do you want?

The objective of these interventions is for the individual to learn how he is interrupting the cycle of need satisfaction at that time, e.g. failing to get the appreciation that he wants.

Gestalt is used for one-to-one work between the trainer and the trainee within the training group. This individual focus, plus the nature of the approach, means that the interventions are always in the high risk area for the individual, the trainer and the group. Although Gestalt is a high risk approach, it is possible to identify a sequence of activity that a trainer could work through with an individual in personal process work. The assumption in this sequence is that in order to work effectively at one level the individual needs to have covered the previous levels, e.g. to invite someone to experiment with expressing his anger when he is not willing to accept that part of himself is clearly a pointless and possibly harmful intervention. The sequence is broadly arranged in order of increasing risk – from becoming aware of a specific behaviour to experimenting with new behaviour.

Levels of Intervention

Increasing awareness of behaviour

The trainer intervenes at the level of 'Pay attention to what you are doing' (to someone who looks agitated). This intervention leaves all of the responsibility for exploration with the course member – and he may respond with silence; a statement about his feelings, e.g. 'I am bored'; or with confusion; 'I don't know what I am doing'. The trainer may slightly raise the risk level by asking him to make an explicit statement: 'What are you doing?'

Fantasy

At this level the trainer focuses on the course member's fears about the consequences of satisfying the underlying need: 'What would happen if you became angry?' The response to such an invitation is likely to be the identification of some catastrophic fantasy, e.g. 'I would become violent'; 'I would destroy you with my anger'; 'You would reject me'. The trainer would then invite the individual to test out reality, e.g. 'I am prepared to take the risk of being destroyed by your anger'.

Making contact

At this level the trainer encourages the course member to make contact with others in the group. This may be in the form of a general invitation: 'Is there anything you would like to say to someone in the group?'; or, a specific suggestion: 'Ask someone here if they would reject you for expressing anger'. The intention here is to allow the course member to feel safer in the group, i.e. by making contact in this way he gives himself permission (and often receives the same permission from others) to be himself in the group.

Exploring the behaviour

At this level the trainer encourages the course member to explore his behaviour. Such invitations may be historical: 'Who told you not to show your anger?'; or, here and now: 'What is your rule about not showing your anger?'. Or it may be an invitation to explore that part of himself via two-chair work: 'Have a dialogue between that angry part of you and the other part of you that represses the anger'. The intention here is for the course member to learn more about himself.

A powerful alternative at this stage is to invite the course member to explore the behaviour through some form of imagery work, e.g. 'Draw a picture of yourself as an angry man'; or to work with any images that the course member uses about himself, e.g.
Course Member: I feel as cold as ice
Trainer: Be the ice – describe yourself to me.

The results of such explorations are exciting, dramatic and effective because in the process of working on the image the individual bypasses many of the blocks and resistances which he may use in other learning situations such as two-chair work, e.g. 'I feel silly talking to an empty chair'.

Exaggerating the behaviour

When exploring an aspect of behaviour the trainer is likely to encourage the course member to exaggerate the behaviour. Such invitations may be verbal: 'Tell someone in the room that you are too frightened to show your anger'; or non-verbal: 'Exaggerate your frightened posture'. The intention here is to encourage the course member to break through the impasse by thoroughly identifying with and owning the repressed feeling.

Experimenting with new behaviour

Having broken through the impasse and expressed the feelings (finishing the business and completing the gestalt) the course member is able to experiment with different ways of managing the feeling. So the trainer is likely to intervene with, 'Find different ways to express your anger at people in this group'. In responding to this intervention the course member is able to discover new choices of behaviour for himself in managing his feelings and relationships.

What determines whether the individual works through this sequence or not is not the skill of the trainer (though this is obviously an important factor) but:

1 The individual's dissatisfaction with what he is doing now;
2 His willingness to learn;
3 His level of support;
     self – physical, emotional and psychological
     external – the trust and acceptance of the trainer and the group.

What often happens is that an individual explores one or more of these levels in one piece of work and wants time to rest and integrate his learning before moving on. At the end of any piece of work the trainer can make valuable interventions by ensuring that integration can take place. This will involve:

1 Inviting the individual to make a clear statement about his desire to stop or go on, in fact, the trainer may need to do this throughout the work.
2 Ensuring that the individual has the necessary support:
     effective breathing – breathing irregularities (catching breath, sighing, holding breath, shallow breathing) are clear indicators that the person is still unfinished, i.e. has not completed the Gestalt. By encouraging him to pay attention to his breathing the trainer can encourage the individual to identify

what he is unfinished about (e.g. he may be still holding on to unexpressed feeling, may not have said all that he has wanted to say etc.)

physical support – another indicator of unfinished business is the individual's physical posture (e.g. perched precariously on a chair). Again, by drawing attention to this the trainer can help the course member to finish outstanding concerns.

feels OK about himself – the third indicator of unfinished business is the course member's difficulty in accepting who he is and what he has done. By asking him how he is feeling now about himself the trainer can identify whether the individual is ready to move on.

3 Ensuring that the individual has the necessary external support from the group and the trainer. This support may involve giving and receiving feed-back and appreciations, or physical contact.

General points

In terms of using the Gestalt approach to personal process work there are some important guidelines that the trainer needs to follow. These guidelines are:

1 If he has any doubts about the risks involved (to the course member or to himself) the trainer should express his concerns and/or hold back from the work. The doubts may be about his own competence in working with the individual or about that person's lack of support systems.

2 The trainer needs to be aware of the danger of following a 'programme' in a piece of work – this 'programme' may be the course member's or the trainer's. Such 'programmes' result from the course member putting himself under pressure to 'perform' (because he believes that this is the price of membership of the group). Or the trainer puts himself under pressure to do an 'effective' piece of work (e.g. to demonstrate his skills in two-chair work).

3 The trainer needs to be clear about his own boundary in relation to the course member. The latter may be presenting an 'issue' which is a live one for the trainer, e.g. the trainer also represses his anger. Where the boundary is confused the danger is that the trainer puts a lot of pressure on the course member to 'resolve' his (the trainer's) issue.

4 As a general guide the trainer is advised to follow what is of interest to the course member; for example

Course Member: I don't want to follow your suggestion.
Trainer: OK, What do you want to do.
This general rule does not preclude the trainer from expressing his own interest in what is happening but the problem of following his own interest is that he will confuse his boundary with the course member and both will end up dissatisfied with their lack of learning.

5 The trainer should be clear about his level of responsibility for the learning (i.e. no more than 50 per cent). This is particularly important when working with individuals who are adept at offering 'seductive' invitations (e.g. 'Do me something', 'Discover me' etc.) which lead to the trainer expending a great deal of energy on them with no return. If in any doubt with an individual the trainer can check his suspicion by asking: 'What do you want?'

References

1 Clark, Neil and Fraser, Tony *The Gestalt Approach: an introduction for managers and trainers*. Roffey Park Management College, 1982.
2 Perls, Frederick S. *In and Out of the Garbage Pail*. Bantam Books, 1972.
3 Herman, S.M. and Korenich, M. *Authentic Management*. Addison-Wesley, 1977

APPENDIX C
EXERCISES

Introduction

It may at first sight appear to be a contradiction in terms that a book on personal process work should include an appendix of exercises. By definition, an exercise means some structure and a movement away from the extreme feeling end of the training spectrum. After some discussion, however, we decided that exercises would be a valuable addition to the book and here are our reasons.

Firstly, the exercises do provide the trainer with an opportunity to work within the feeling area, even though he may not get involved in personal process work. Many of the exercises we have included here do provide a bridge between the pure doing approach and the feeling approach. The exercises are a lower risk way of exploring feelings, as compared, for example, with a 'here and now' examination of individual and group processes.

A second and related point is that the exercises can generate material and awareness which can lead to personal process work. This might take place in the review of the exercise, or could happen at a later stage. Since trust and support are important pre-conditions for personal process work, these exercises can be used to generate such an atmosphere. Also the trainer through such exercises can do some testing of feelings within the group and therefore have more data for deciding about the appropriateness of personal process work.

Our third and final point has already been implicitly dealt with above. Exercises can be important not only for the development of the trainee, but also the trainer. They can be handled in different ways with different styles and help the trainer become clearer about his own personal and professional boundaries and whether he could/should push them. Indeed the exercises can be used to develop the training team where they can be tested out and reviewed at a number of levels (e.g. the mechanics of handling and briefing, personal learning, learning about others, and training ethics).

THE EXERCISES

They fall broadly into five categories:

1 Introductory Exercises (1 and 2)

These involve implicit and explicit process interventions, but rarely lead to any significant personal process work. Their importance lies in the expectations and understanding they raise about the nature of the course, and the indirect opportunities they may provide for follow up later on in the programme.

2 Feedback Exercises (3 – 5)

These are central to any semi-structured programme which has a 'here and now' focus. The exercises are frequently used to raise awareness as a step leading to personal process work.

3 Influencing, Assertion and non-Verbal Exercises (6 – 11)

As with feedback exercises, these are powerful ways of leading into personal process work. They also reflect areas of increasing interest to organisations and course members alike.

4 Theory-based Exercises (12 – 19)

These are exercises to illustrate and build on particular concepts that are very likely to be particularly relevant to personal process work.

5 'Organisational' Exercises (20 and 21)

These illustrate concepts with wider organisational implications, but can also be reviewed in such a way as to lead into personal process work.

These categories are not mutually exclusive but do reflect the emphases which we would generally put on them.

Throughout the description of the exercises, the following assumptions are made:

1 The course is about five days long, and residential
2 The maximum number of participants is 12
3 The course is concerned either with the general development of interpersonal skills or with the development of specific skills such as influencing and counselling.

With shorter courses and more participants, higher risk exercises (and consequently the scope for introducing personal process work) are less suitable. This is particularly so where the training is non-residential.

Each exercise is organised under the following headings:

Title
Aims
Numbers of participants
Length of exercise (including review)
Timing on the course
Briefing (i.e. instruction details)
Commentary (i.e. brief comments on such issues as risk levels, variations or other points of interest).

The length stated for each exercise is approximate, and is particularly unpredictable if the review leads into personal process work. Where odd numbers of participants are concerned, adjustments to the numbers and the structures of the exercises are needed.

The judgements of risk level are approximate only, based on our experience. Clearly, in the final analysis what is low risk for one participant may be high for another. Having said that, points regarding the management of risk occur frequently in the main body of this book and are closely linked with the trainers' decisions regarding implicit and explicit process interventions. Any of the exercises could lead to personal process work although for this to happen several factors would need to be taken into account, not least of which would be aims of the training itself.

In terms of their source, some of the exercises are original, and others are closely related to existing ones widely used by a number of trainers. It is in the nature of training exercises that they often pass into common usage without a clear knowledge of who actually created them. Certainly the reader is welcome to adapt these exercises to meet his own needs. It is important that a trainer uses such exercises in a way that feels comfortable and works for him and his participants, rather than sticking rigidly to the stated format.

EXERCISE 1 : NEEDS AND GIFTS

Aims

1 To provide a means for participants to get to know one other person in the group;
2 To share things about themselves as people (needs, wants, qualities, attributes and feelings) rather than their roles (i.e. job details);
3 To provide a vehicle for personal introductions to the whole course group;
4 To provide an opportunity for participants and trainers to clarify expectations about the course.

Numbers

Pairs

Length

1 hour 15 minutes to 1 hour 30 minutes

Timing

At the beginning of a course.

Briefing

1 Each participant is given a large envelope, pen and blank piece of paper.
2 Each individual then takes five minutes to write down on the outside of the envelope a statement of needs and wants for the course (e.g. new skills, involvement, fun), and also a statement of current feelings (e.g. excitement, apprehension, cynicism).
3 Each person then takes another 5 minutes to write down on the piece of paper any gifts (e.g. particular knowledge, experience, personal qualities) they would like to offer their partner and the course. This paper is then placed inside the envelope.
4 The participants form pairs, exchange envelopes and take 15 minutes talking to each other on the basis of the envelopes.
5 When ready, each person introduces his partner to the whole group, using the information discussed.

6   The trainer(s) introduce himself/themselves similarly, and use the introductions for clarifying the expectations of the course.

Commentary

Risk level is fairly high since most people come to courses expecting to introduce themselves on the basis of role, organisation and work experience. For this reason it is important that the trainers introduce themselves in a similar way (i.e. make an implicit process intervention). It may even be valuable for one of the trainers to go first so as to provide a model. Steps 1 and 2 in the briefing (with the idea of gifts for the participants to offer) underline the shared nature of the responsibility for learning. There are many variations to the exercise, e.g. listing the points on a flip chart, working in trios. An obvious activity following this exercise would be to present and discuss the nature of the course.

EXERCISE 2: FIRST IMPRESSIONS

Aims

1   To give course members the opportunity to become aware of their first impressions;
2   To test the assumptions on which their first impressions are based;
3   To develop skills in observing and giving feedback.

Numbers

Trios, working in separate rooms.

Length

1 hour 15 minutes to 1 hour 30 minutes.

Timing

Late on Day 1 of the course

Briefing

1   Participants form into trios.

2   Each participant takes it in turn to give their personal
     impressions of their two partners for up to 15 minutes.
     Suitable areas for observation and feedback include:
     (a)   appearance (clothing and dress, build)
     (b)   non-verbal behaviour (posture, gestures, movement,
           facial expressions, eye contact, breathing)
     (c)   speech (accent, tone, quality, speed, content)
     (d)   attitudes   and   feelings   (openness,   shyness,
           confidence, anxiety etc.)
     Participants are given the following guidelines for the
     activity.
     (a)   to be as honest and open as they can
     (b)   to make sure they understand what they hear,
           without necessarily accepting it
     (c)   to take their time checking the impressions against
           their own experiences of themselves.
3   Each trio takes the opportunity to raise any general or specific
     points from their experiences in step 2 in a full group review.

Commentary

The risk level is high since many people are reluctant to exchange first
impressions in their daily lives. Consequently the most appropriate
place to do the exercise is after introductions and one, perhaps two,
lower risk exercises (e.g. 'there and then' syndicate discussions) so
that participants have started to get to know one another. Obviously
leaving it much later would reduce its relevance since people would
have started forming second and third impressions.

This exercise is based on the importance of first impressions to both
the quality and process of relationships generally, and is of particular
relevance to organisational roles (e.g. salesmen). Apart from reviewing the learning of the participants, and raising any theoretical
aspects, the trainer may invite participants to share first impressions
of him.

EXERCISE 3: TRIOS FEEDBACK

Aims

1   To provide participants with an opportunity to receive feed-
     back;

2   To explore how they respond to feedback;
3   To examine the nature of feedback, including ways of giving and receiving it.

Numbers

Trios

Length

1 hour 15 minutes

Timing

Day 2 or early on Day 3

Briefing

1   Participants form into trios and label themselves A, B and C. A is the giver of feedback, B is the receiver, and C the observer.
2   A starts by giving feedback to B that is real and 'significant'; i.e. it could provide some important learning. A decides the content (what aspect of B's behaviour to give feedback on) and the form (descriptive or evaluative, positive or negative, etc.). B responds in whatever way makes sense to him. C observes the *process* and comments *how* the feedback was given and received.
3   A, B and C then switch roles so that they all have the opportunity to give and receive feedback, and observe.
4   Each trio raises any general or specific points in a concluding full group review.

Commentary

The risk level is variable with much scope for participants to work at a variety of levels. The exercise makes a good introduction to feedback. As a preliminary step, a theory session on the relevance of feedback to personal awareness and interpersonal skill development, including ways of giving and receiving feedback, needs to be provided. Again, there are many variations, including working in pairs without an observer.

EXERCISE 4: APPRECIATIONS AND CONSIDERATIONS

Aims

1 To provide participants with an opportunity to give and receive positive feedback;
2 To provide participants with an opportunity to give and receive negative feedback, presented in as constructive and supportive way as possible.

Numbers

Up to 12 participants, plus one or two tutors, seated in a circle.

Length

45 minutes to 1 hour

Timing

Day 4

Briefing

1 The trainer places a pen or stick on the floor in the middle of the circle.
2 Whoever wants to is invited to start by:
   (a) picking up the pen;
   (b) addressing another person in the group with 'What I appreciate about you is . . . ' followed by, 'and what I would like you to consider is . . . ' (i.e. suggesting some change or modification of behaviour)
3 The giver of feedback then passes the pen to the receiver.
4 The receiver takes a few seconds to reflect on the feedback and may ask for clarification only.
5 The receiver then repeats steps 2 and 3 with another member of the group, and so on.

Commentary

The risk level is relatively high, and the exercise depends on the participants and trainers having a good deal of information and experience of one another. The exercise is a very good closing activity for Day 4, bearing in mind the time required to clear down any unfinished business and any related personal process work. Variations include restricting the feedback to all appreciations or all considerations.

EXERCISE 5 : TRIOS SCULPTURE

Aims

1 To provide course members with an opportunity to give and receive feedback non-verbally;
2 To explore aspects of non-verbal behaviour.

Numbers

Trios

Length

45 minutes to 1 hour 15 minutes

Timing

Day 4

Briefing

1 Participants form into trios and label themselves A, B and C.
2 The As start by taking 2 minutes physically to position the Bs and Cs into postures, gestures and facial expressions that reflect A's experience of them during the course. Props, such as chairs, may be used.
3 The Bs and Cs take two minutes to reflect on their impressions and interpretations of the postures in which they have been placed.
4 The Bs then take the initiative in positioning the other two (steps 2 and 3) followed by the Cs.
5 The experience is reviewed in the total group.

Commentary

The risk level is high, principally because of the physical contact involved. A variant of the exercise is the large group sculpture where one individual positions the rest of the course group. The idea underlying the exercise is to 'undercut' the complexities and avoidances often present in verbal feedback. The exercise therefore encapsulates an item of feedback which, if expressed verbally, could be rather confused and confusing.

EXERCISE 6: ABILITIES AND ASSERTION

Aims

1 To provide a first step in exploring assertion by inviting participants to reflect on their abilities, strengths and achievements, i.e. where they have asserted themselves in their lives;
2 To provide participants with an opportunity to explore this on a process level, through their feelings as they talk about themselves, and through the observations and feedback of others in the group.

Numbers

Groups of 4 in separate rooms

Length

1 hour to 1 hour 15 minutes

Timing

Day 2 or Day 3

Briefing

1 Each person takes up to 20 minutes to write down his answers to the following questions.

What natural abilities do I have?
What things do I do better than most people?
What are the most difficult things I have accomplished in my life?
What am I most proud of?

2 The course members form into small groups of four.
3 Each person takes it in turn to read out his answers. Whilst doing this, he pays attention to his feelings (e.g. pride, embarrassment) and style (e.g. censoring, distorting). The listeners pay attention to the speaker's non-verbal behaviour.

4 The speaker and listeners discuss their experiences and observations.
5 Steps 3 and 4 are repeated by the remainder of the quartet.
6 The activity is discussed in the full group.

Commentary

This is a medium risk activity to the extent that people may see themselves as being asked to brag or boast and hence possibly break personal rules about modesty. It is a good first exercise in assertion and related to self-stroking, (see Appendix A on TA). There is the option of a theory input on influencing and assertion to take place before or after. It is partly 'there and then' and partly 'here and now', and the trainer has a clear choice to stay with the former or to increase the risk level by making explicit process interventions about the latter.

EXERCISE 7 : 'SMILES'

Aims

To examine a range of behaviours available for influencing, including the choices, limitations, and recurring patterns used by participants.

Numbers

Pairs

Length

30 minutes

Timing

Day 2

Briefing

1 Participants pick partners and label themselves A and B.
2 A finds as many ways as possible to influence B to smile,

without using physical contact. The task of B is to respond genuinely to the behaviour of A.

3   At the end of 5 minutes, B gives A feedback on:
    (a) what he responded to;
    (b) what he found easy to resist.

4   A and B then reverse roles. On completion participants identify any characteristics of influencing and being influenced that they are willing to discuss in the full group.

5   Full group review.

Commentary

This is a medium risk exercise which explores some of the subtle influencing behaviours, together with the potency of personal rules in limiting individual options.

A key component in the briefing for this exercise is to invite the group to have fun and be creative, and not 'try too hard'.

A good starting point for the full group review is for the trainer to ask what difficulties individuals experienced during the exercise (e.g. getting started, artificial etc.) with a view to exploring the limits they impose on themselves in other influencing situations.

EXERCISE 8 : REVERSING AND MIRRORING

Aims

1   To illustrate the importance of non-verbal behaviour in communication;
2   To highlight the consequences of double messages;
3   To develop participants' skills in establishing rapport by mirroring non-verbal behaviour;
4   To develop awareness of own and others' behaviour.

Numbers

Pairs

Length

30–45 minutes

Timing

Day 2

Briefing

1 Participants form pairs and label themselves A and B.
2 The task of A is to talk about a hobby or interest for no more than 5 minutes. The task of B is to respond at the content level, as in a normal conversation, but to demonstrate the reverse of all the non-verbal behaviours of A. For example:

    if A smiles, B frowns;

    if A leans forward, B sits back in the chair;

    if A talks in a soft tone of voice, B talks in a loud tone.

3 At the end of 5 minutes the pairs share their experiences with each other, especially how easy or difficult it was to maintain the conversation over 5 minutes and the impact that different non-verbal behaviours had on the conversation.
4 Step 2 is repeated with A still talking about a hobby or interest for no more than 5 minutes. This time B mirrors all the non-verbal behaviours of A, as well as responding to the content. For example;

    if A smiles, B smiles etc.

5 Step 3 is then repeated.
6 The pairs raise any general or specific points from their experiences in a concluding full group interview.

Commentary

The risk level in this exercise will probably be reduced by the trainer briefing the group to enjoy themselves and be creative. It can be used on counselling skills courses to focus on mirroring as a particular skill in developing rapport between counsellor and client.

EXERCISE 9 : CHAIRS

Aims

1 To explore the range of influencing styles;
2 To enable participants to check/confirm their dominant influencing styles and discover ones they rarely or never use;
3 To develop people's awareness of how they are influenced by others.

Numbers

Groups of four

Length

45 minutes to 1 hour 14 minutes

Timing

Day 2 or 3

Briefing

1 Participants form into groups of 4
2 One member of each quartet then volunteers to start the activity
3 The other 3 people sit on chairs, with the volunteer standing in front of them.
4 He then attempts to influence one of the seated people to give up his chair. All means may be used, including physical contact, apart from the potentially harmful or obviously offensive. It is important that none of those seated is 'unreasonably' stubborn, and allows himself to be open to influence.
5 Once someone has given up his chair, he then takes his turn in influencing someone else to relinquish his.
6 At the end of 15 minutes, each quartet spends another 5–10 minutes discussing:
    (a) 'successes' – 'failures'
    (b) who gave up his chair and why
    (c) who did not – why
    (d) what approaches were not tried
7 The exercise is completed with a large group review.

Commentary

The exercise can generate much noise and fun and may be useful as an energiser. If used in this way the risk level is likely to be quite low. Variations include:
    (a) excluding the use of physical contact
    (b) the trainer intervening to help anyone who is stuck
    (c) doing the exercise in the whole group, though this is higher risk as individuals may feel more exposed.
An important theoretical input from the trainer before or after the exercise is to describe a range of influencing approaches, including ethical considerations. These approaches can be integrated with a TA framework (see Appendix A).

EXERCISE 10 : TRUTH AND DISTORTION

Aims

1   To develop skills in observing, particularly in recognising non-verbal indicators of deception, exaggeration or minimising;
2   To develop skills in handling situations where the 'truth' is being distorted by another party.

Numbers

Groups of 3 to 5, in separate rooms

Length

45 minutes to 1 hour

Timing

Day 2 or 3

Briefing

1   Participants form groups of 3 to 5.
2   One person describes to the rest of his group a successful, catastrophic or exciting event in which he was involved, at work or elsewhere. The speaker's task is to deceive his colleagues by frequently lying, exaggerating or minimising some aspects of the story. The listeners' task is
    (a)   to point out lying, exaggerating or minimising
    (b)   to describe *how* they recognise these things
    (c)   to produce a list providing a guide to the recognition of these behaviours
3   Repeat step 2 with two other people
4   Discuss and establish
    (a)   who was successful and why
    (b)   who was unsuccessful and why
    (c)   what skills are needed to confront deception, exaggeration or minimisation.

Commentary

We would regard it as unethical if this exercise were used to help people be more successful in deceiving others. The exercise clearly raises issues about deception and manipulation and the trainer needs to be clear with himself and the group about his position in these issues, e.g. is deception an appropriate choice?

EXERCISE 11 : AVOID SENDING A MESSAGE
Aims

1 To increase skills in observation;
2 To demonstrate the considerable difficulty in *not* sending non-verbal messages to other people.

Numbers

Pairs

Length

20 minutes maximum

Timing

Day 1 onwards

Briefing

1 The group form pairs, label themselves A and B, and sit opposite each other, with no tables in between.
2 The task of A is to spend two minutes in consciously *not* expressing any non-verbal behaviour to B.
3 The task of B is to note all the non-verbal behaviour expressed by B; e.g. eye contact, facial expressions, changes in muscle tension, changes in breathing patterns, even 'twitches and spasms'.
4 After two minutes, the roles are reversed.
5 The pairs discuss their observations for three minutes.
6 The activity is reviewed in the total group.

Commentary

This exercise is a simple, low risk 'fun' activity that can be used very early in a course to start exploring non-verbal behaviour in relationships. It is unlikely to raise many options for personal process work but forms a useful contrast to Exercise 5. Some theory on non-verbal behaviour is a useful follow up.

EXERCISE 12 : LIFE POSITIONS

Aims

1   To give participants an opportunity to relate the concept of life
    positions (see Appendix A) to themselves;
2   To identify personal choices in collaborating and competing
    with others.

Numbers

Pairs, in separate rooms

Length

1 hour to 1 hour 30 minutes

Timing

Day 3 or 4

Briefing

1   The group forms pairs.
2   One person starts and gives feedback to the others on the basis
    of the life positions, i.e. how and over what issue he feels
    $1 + U +$, $1 + U-$, $1-U+$, $1-U-$ in relation to his partner. A
    suitable format is 'I feel $1+U+$ in relation to you because . . . '
    The issues concerned do not have to be big, and may be based
    on a 'small' fleeting moment.
    It is important that the recipient seeks clarification but does not
    justify.
3   The pairs switch roles.
4   The pairs raise any key general or specific points in a
    concluding group review.

Commentary

This can be a high risk exercise, and an even higher risk variation is to
do this as a whole group activity. Another variant is to use trios, with
the third party acting as observer and helper. It is not advisable to run
this exercise in the early part of a course not only because of the risk
level but also because of the experience of one another that people will
need. It can be used when the trainer has reason to believe that there
are a lot of unresolved issues in the group.

EXERCISE 13: SOCIODRAMA TRIANGLE

Aim

To give and receive feedback based on the concept of the drama triangle roles (see Appendix A), as perceived and experienced by course members

Numbers

The whole group

Length

1 to 1½ hours

Timing

Late on Day 2 onwards

Briefing

1   The trainer places three sheets of paper on the floor at the corners of a triangle, to represent the drama triangle. One sheet is labelled P (for persecutor), one R (for rescuer) and one V (for victim).

2   The trainer invites a volunteer from the course to position the remainder of the group on or near what he believes are their dominant drama triangle positions. His decision may be based on his experience and/or intuition. The group are requested not to talk during this stage.

3   After this positioning, the rest of the group are invited to seek verbal feedback, including reasons and clarification from the initiator, without entering into justifications. They are also encouraged to express their own feelings and views about their positions.

4   Other volunteers may repeat steps 2 and 3 to provide differing perspectives.

Commentary

This exercise needs to follow a theoretical presentation, perhaps with some form of individual self assessment of preferred positions. It is inherently a high risk exercise, needing a good deal of trust by all concerned. This is largely because of the judgemental qualities associated with the roles. It is important for the trainer to stress that they are not 'global' statements of all of an individual's behaviour. The trainer himself may well be invited to give his views, and this can be useful in clarifying his role in the group.

EXERCISE 14 : HAVE TO/CHOOSE TO
Aims

1　For participants to identify some of their Parent messages (see Appendix A) and/or introjects (see Appendix B);
2　To explore the personal impact of these messages and/or introjects.

Numbers

Pairs

Length

1 hour 30 minutes

Timing

Day 2 onwards

Briefing

1　Participants spend up to 10 minutes writing down a series of five to ten statements beginning
　　In my life I have to . . . ; e.g. be nice to people; always to be right; etc.
2　Participants then spend up to a further 10 minutes writing against each statement a further statement 'or else . . . '; e.g. people won't accept me; I will have failed; etc.
3　Participants form pairs and
　　(a)　first share their lists
　　(b)　then rephrase each statement into 'I choose to . . . because . . . '
　　While each individual is undertaking this activity, they work with their partner to
　　(c)　establish clarity
　　(d)　gain further feedback

(e) modify their 'rules', i.e. statements so as to make them
     less limiting and self-defeating for each individual.
4   The pairs raise any specific or general points in a full group
    review.

Commentary

This exercise has both a TA and a Gestalt basis, so either of these
models can be used to provide a theoretical background.

EXERCISE 15 : INTERNAL PROCESS/EXTERNAL BEHAVIOUR

Aims

1 To provide an opportunity for participants to discover how
   their internal process affects and limits their external behaviour
   and hence their options for relating to and influencing others;
2 To use this knowledge in making new decisions for relating to
   and influencing others.

Numbers

Pairs

Length

1 hour 15 minutes to 1 hour 30 minutes

Timing

Day 3 onwards

Briefing

1 Participants take up to 10 minutes individually to identify up to
   five specific behaviours which they have used during the week.
   These behaviours may be old 'patterns' or new 'experiments',
   and are listed in the right hand column as shown below.

   Internal process   *External behaviour*
   Feelings   e.g. Initiating conversation
   Thoughts   Asking for feedback
   Rules and Beliefs   Smiling
                                   Always going last
                                   Attacking others etc.

2   Participants form pairs labelled A and B.
3   A describes the incident(s) in which he used each behaviour and, with the help of B asking questions, A explores:
    (a)   his feelings at the time; e.g. 'I was uncomfortable'.
    (b)   his thoughts at the time; e.g. 'I was saying to myself "Don't be foolish! "'
    (c)   whether the behaviour was compatible with or in conflict with any rules he has about how to behave; e.g. 'I must not be critical of others'.
        A lists these points in the left hand column as shown above.
4   On completing this explanation A considers one or more decisions about how to use the behaviour(s) in the future; e.g. 'I will practise being assertive with people who are a low risk for me'. A takes 20 minutes for steps 3 and 4.
5   A and B then reverse roles and go through steps 3 and 4 for a further 20 minutes.
6   The pairs raise any specific or general points in a concluding large group review.

Commentary

This exercise is based on the frequent need for people to look at both internal process and external behaviour when exploring patterns in their relationships. The use of pairings makes the exercise low to medium risk. However, the whole group review becomes higher risk if an individual raises issues about his internal process, and the trainer will then need to consider the appropriateness of inviting the person into personal process work.

EXERCISE 16 : AWARENESS CONTINUUM

Aim

To heighten awareness of internal processes, feelings and external events.

Numbers

Pairs

Length

15 to 20 minutes

Timing

Day 1 onwards

Briefing

1   Participants form pairs, sit opposite each other, and designate themselves A and B.
2   A starts by making a series of statements to B, beginning; 'Now I am aware of . . . '; e.g. 'my back aching, the traffic outside, you're starting to smile' etc.
3   After 2 minutes, B offers A any comments or feedback and then the pair reverse roles.
4   Pairs raise any specific or general points in a concluding total group review

Commentary

This is a paired version of *the* basic Gestalt awareness exercise. By definition it is designed to increase awareness and can be very useful for those groups where the participants are simply unaccustomed to paying attention to the details of their feelings, their posture and the world around them.

EXERCISE 17 : DRAW AN OBJECT

Aim

For participants to increase their self-awareness.

Numbers

Whole group

Length

Up to 3 hours

Timing

Day 4

Briefing

1 Each course member is given a sheet of flip chart paper and a felt tip pen and asked to draw a picture of an object that in some way represents who he is and how he is feeling at the moment.

2 Each person in turn then presents his drawing to the group by describing himself as the object. Each sentence of his description must be made in the first person e.g.

'I am . . . '
'I have . . . '
'I feel . . . '

3 At the end of each presentation, the other participants take time to offer feedback of their experiences of the picture and their feelings about the person while it was being presented.

Commentary

This also is a Gestalt awareness activity. It is high risk for three reasons:

1 It is very unusual in terms of most people's learning experience; e.g. use of images.

2 It takes place in the whole group.

3 During each person's presentation, the trainer invites the course member to engage in personal process work. He will be following as much as leading and cannot be certain of the underlying issue which the picture represents.

Furthermore, it is beneficial to have two trainers present during the exercise, since it can be a highly emotional experience. Certainly, no participant should be forced to present his picture against his will.

EXERCISE 18 : INTROJECTIONS

Aims

1   To provide participants with an opportunity to identify some of their introjects (see Appendix B);
2   To discover the impact of these introjects on the participants' behaviour in groups, and their approach to learning.

Numbers

Whole group

Length

1 hour

Timing

Day 3

Briefing

1   Participants take up to 10 minutes to write down the 'rules' they have for being a member of the course group, including ones they may have broken. Participants are asked to write these rules in terms of:
    'I should . . . '
    'I must . . . '
    'I ought . . . '
2   When ready, participants take it in turns to 'put' their rules out on to other members of the group e.g. 'Terry, you should pay attention in this group'. If the group is large and the rules many, participants are encouraged to be selective, e.g. putting out only one of their rules to each person.
3   The exercise is concluded with a full group review, including
    (a)   the relevance and importance of the introjects to individuals
    (b)   the consequence of the introjects to the progress of the course
    (c)   how the person felt when turning the rules outwards.

Commentary

This is a medium risk exercise, which provides an opportunity for individuals to explore the current validity of their introjects.

EXERCISE 19 : PROJECTIONS

Aim

To provide participants with an opportunity to identify some of their projections (see Appendix B).

Numbers

Pairs

Length

45 minutes to 1 hour

Timing

Day 3

Briefing

1   Participants are asked to think of someone current or past that they like very much, and take 5 minutes to list the qualities and attributes of that person.
2   They are then asked to repeat the activity for someone current or past that they dislike intensely.
3   In pairs, the course members take it in turns to 'own' the listed qualities by saying to their partner 'I am, sad, angry, caring, condescending, etc. As they do this, each individual checks out with himself, and his partner, which statements make sense and which are difficult to accept.
4   The exercise is completed with a full group review.

Commentary

This is a high risk exercise which can be done in groups of three or four, or even the whole group (with a correspondingly increased risk). It provides many opportunities for learning, insight, and feedback from others in the group.

EXERCISE 20 : GROUP BOUNDARIES

Aim

To provide an opportunity to explore boundary issues in a group.

Numbers

Whole group

Length

1 hour 30 minutes

Timing

Late on Day 2 onwards

Briefing

1 The whole group are asked to stand up, moving any chairs or desks out of the way.
2 One individual is invited to position the rest of the group around the room, either singly or in small groups, according to his own criteria. Examples might include:
    (a)   physical similarities
    (b)   common interests and backgrounds
    (c)   'cliques'
    (d)   assertive and non-assertive people
    (e)   those working with the material and those resisting etc.
During this step no one is allowed to talk.
3 The individual then explains his criteria.
4 The rest of the group are then given an opportunity to respond and seek clarification.
5 The activity is repeated at least one more time.

Commentary

This is a medium risk exercise because of its physical nature, and the risk level can be high for the individuals doing the positioning. For this reason it is a good idea to involve the trainers in the positioning as well. The exercise will probably need to be preceded by a brief in-put on boundaries and their possible implications for individuals and groups.

EXERCISE 21 : ORGANISATION CULTURE

Aims

1 For participants from the same organisation to share and compare perceptions of their organisation;
2 For participants to pursue the development of new skills, and have fun at the same time.

Numbers

Course group split into two, and working in separate rooms.

Length

2–3 hours

Timing

Day 3 or 4

Briefing

1 The group is split into two.
2 The task of each group is to make a statement which reflects the sub-group's perception of their organisation. Ways of making this statement include:
   (a) a short play (say 10 minutes)
   (b) a group sculpt (see Exercise 5)
   (c) drawing one or more pictures
   (e) writing and presenting a poem or a song
Suitable resources are made available to the groups, e.g. paper, pens, photocopying facilities, closed-circuit television, tape recorders etc.
3 Participants are encouraged to pay attention to their process during the activity, practise and develop new skills, and to be creative and have fun.
4 After the presentations, the groups and trainer(s) review the content and the process of the activities.

Commentary

As described above, this exercise can only be used with in-company courses. The exercise is valuable as an energiser, and is variable in its risk level. The review provides scope for fairly low risk interventions, and personal process work, for example in the light of an individual receiving personal feedback on his role and contribution to the activity.

FURTHER READING

INTERPERSONAL SKILLS TRAINING
(Chapters 1 & 2)

Boshear, Walton C. & Albrecht, Karl G., *Understanding People: Models and Concepts* University Associates, (paperback) 1977. pp. 275.
Concise descriptions of models and concepts which aid understanding of the individual, pairs, groups, organisations and problem-solving.

Cooper, Cary L. ed., *Improving Interpersonal Relations: some approaches to social skills training* Gower, 1981. pp. 129.
Chapters on TA, Interaction Analysis, Assertiveness and the T-Group.

Cooper, Cary L. ed., *Hurt or Helped?: a study of the personal impact on managers of experiential small group training programmes.* HMSO (paperback) 1977. pp. 45.
Results of research into 12 training programmes over 18 months.

Heron, John, *Dimensions of Facilitator Style* Human Potential Research Project, University of Surrey (paperback) 1977. pp. 50
Paper based on workshops run by Heron. Contains six-dimension model of facilitator style.

Phillips, Keri & Fraser, Tony, *The Management of Interpersonal Skills Training* Gower, 1982. pp. 224
Provides a framework which compares and distinguishes the main approaches and examines such problems as designing and running courses, the management of feedback activities.

Rackham, Neil, Honey, Peter and Colbert, Michael, *Developing Interactive Skills* Wellens Publishing, 1971. pp. 191
Includes a survey of different approaches to training and outlines the development of their own approach.

Smith, Peter, *Group Processes and Personal Change* Harper and Row (paperback), 1980. pp. 257.
Examines different forms of group training (e.g. Encounter, Tavistock, etc.) with chapters on the learning process and the effects of the training.

FEELING-BASED APPROACHES TO INTERPERSONAL SKILLS TRAINING (Chapters 3 & 4)

Transactional Analysis

Barker, Dave, *TA and Training: the theory and use of TA in organisations* Gower, 1980. pp. 225.
Includes the theory and its application in a variety of training situations along the thinking, doing, feeling spectrum.

Barker, Dave & Phillips, Keri, *T.A.: a basic introduction for the manager* Roffey Park Management College (paperback), 1981. pp. 34.
Brief description of the theory; its use as a training aid; and some training exercises.

Berne, Eric, *What do you say after you say 'Hello?': the psychology of human destiny* Corgi, (paperback), 1975. pp. 456.
Contains a chapter on the basic concepts, but is primarily concerned with describing and analysing different life scripts.

Harris, Thomas H., *I'm OK – You're OK* Pan Books (paperback), 1973. pp. 269.
General introduction to the theory and its implications for some wider aspects of society and human existence.

James, Muriel & Jongeward, Dorothy, *Born to Win: T.A. with some Gestalt experiments* Signet, New York (paperback), 1978. pp. 329.
An introductory book, reviewing the theory and its application in everyday life, together with some Gestalt training exercises.

Klein, Mavis, *Lives People Live: a textbook of T.A.* John Wiley (paperback), 1980. pp. 183.
Arranged in three sections: theory, diagnosis and therapy.

[handwritten: ADVANCED TA]

Steiner, Claude M., *Scripts People Live: Transactional Analysis of Life Scripts* Bantam Books, New York (paperback), 1975. pp. 394.
A detailed analysis of script theory; including male and female scripts; therapy related to scripts; the idea of TA contracts and a mini-biography of Eric Berne.

Gestalt *[handwritten: underlying approach of IRO)2 course, course between]*

Clark, Neil and Fraser, Tony, *The Gestalt Approach: an introduction for managers and trainers* Roffey Park Management College (paperback), 1982. pp. 42.
Covers origins of Gestalt, description of basic theory, its application in training, and personal exercises.

Herman, Stanley M. and Korenich, Michael, *Authentic Management: a Gestalt orientation to organisations and their development* Addison-Wesley (paperback), 1977. pp. 236.
Describes some of the theory and relates it to issues in organisational life. Also contains exercises, case studies, and identifies key issues in consultancy.

Perls, Frederick S. ('Fritz'), *The Gestalt Approach and Eyewitness to Therapy* Bantam Books (paperback), 1976. pp. 209.
Two books in one volume – a readable introduction to the theory, and transcripts of training films.

Perls, Frederick S. ('Fritz') *Gestalt Therapy Verbatim* Bantam Books (paperback), 1971. pp. 306.
Transcripts of seminars and workshops run by Perls at the Esalen Institute from 1966 to 1968.

Perls, Frederick S., Hefferline, Ralph F. & Goodman, Paul, *Gestalt Therapy: excitement and growth in the human personality* Pelican (paperback), 1973. pp. 535.
The standard work on Gestalt. Contains a series of experiments. Recommended for readers who already have some knowledge and understanding of the basic concepts.

Simkin, James S., *Gestalt Therapy Mini-Lectures* Celestial Arts, California (paperback), 1976, pp. 124.
Good and readable book – particularly useful for the trainer involved in any approach to feeling-based training.

Other Approaches

Bion, W.R., *Experiences in Groups: and other papers* Tavistock

(paperback), 1968. pp. 198.
Description of the 'Tavistock Approach' to group training.

Blatner, Howard A., *Acting-in: practical applications of Psychodramatic Methods* Springer Publishing Company, New York (paperback), 1973. pp. 152.
Description of the theory, the process and roles; applications of the methods; training the trainer; brief history of the approach, and a biography of Moreno.

Bradford, Leland P., Gibb, Jack R. & Benne, Kenneth D., *The T-Group Theory and Laboratory Method: innovation in re-education* Wiley, 1964. pp. 498.
Describes the origins, development and use of T-group training.

Lankton, Steve, *Practical Magic: a translation of basic Neuro-Linguistic into clinical psychotherapy*. Meto Publications, California. 1980. pp. 250.
Description of the origins, theory, and applications of NLP.

Lowen, Alexander *Bioenergetics* Penguin (paperback), 1976. pp. 352.
Description of the approach which involves releasing physical tensions in the body. Includes theory and exercises.

Proctor, Brigid, *Counselling Shop: an introduction to the theories and techniques of ten approaches to counselling* Burnett Books, 1978. pp. 297.
Includes Rogerian, TA, Gestalt and co-counselling. Detailed and concise description of the approaches.

Rogers, Carl R., *Encounter Groups* Pelican (paperback), 1973. pp. 174.
An approach which uses a number of standard physical contact exercises for developing awareness.

Schutz, William C., *Joy: expanding human awareness* Pelican (paperback), 1967. pp. 189.
Development and management of Encounter Groups by their founder.

HUMANISTIC PSYCHOLOGY (Chapter 5)

Bugenthal, James T. ed., *Challenges of Humanistic Psychology* McGraw-Hill (paperback), 1967. pp. 362.

Origins, development, review of some research, and a description of some of the approaches.

Dychtwald, Ken, *Body – Mind* Jove Books, New York (paperback), 1978. pp. 299.
Offers a comprehensive system for developing an understanding of the mind-body relationship. Draws on a number of approaches; Bioenergetics, Rolfing, Reich, etc.

Ernst, Sheila & Goodison, Lucy, *In Our Own Hands: a book of self-help therapy* Women's Press (paperback), 1981. pp. 328.
Guide to some current approaches – with a critique of each based on feminist and socialist values. Offers advice to individuals who want to enter groups and to those who want to start their own groups. Also includes exercises.

Kovel, Joel, *A Complete Guide to Therapy* Pelican, 1978. pp. 369.
Includes analytical and post-analytical approaches. Also offers a guide for the perplexed.

Otto, Herbert A. and Mann, J., *Ways of Growth: approaches to expanding awareness* Viking Press, New York. (paperback), 1968. pp. 227.
Brief description of some of the approaches; Gestalt, Encounter, dreams, meditation etc.

Rowan, John, *Ordinary Ecstasy: humanistic psychology in action* Routledge and Kegan Paul (paperback), 1976. pp. 234.
Origins, eight areas of application (e.g. counselling, education, organisational etc), and looks at the implications for both the individual and society.

Shaffer, John B.P., *Humanistic Psychology* Prentice-Hall (paperback), 1978. pp. 198.
Origins and development, with descriptions of some of the approaches.

Shaffer, John B.P. and Galinsky, M. David, *Models of Group Therapy and Sensitivity Training* Prentice-Hall, 1974. pp. 303.
Detailed descriptions of Encounter, T-Groups, Psychodrama, Gestalt, Tavistock and other approaches.

Wyckoff, Hogie, *Solving Women's Problems: through awareness, action and contact* Grove Press, New York. (paperback), 1977. pp. 269.

Handbook for women who wish to organise their own problem-solving group. Strong emphasis on TA as an approach.

THE TRAINER (Chapter 6)

Training Exercises

Adair, John et al., *A Handbook of Management Training Exercises* 2 vols. BACIE (ring-binders), 1980–82. pp. 160. pp. 132.
Volume 1 contains 25 exercises with background notes; volume 2 contains references to the background notes.

Brandes, Donna and Phillips, Howard, *Gamesters Handbook: 140 games for teachers and group leaders* Hutchinson (paperback), 1978. pp. 154.
Exercises arranged in four sections – social development, personal development, concentrative (focusing), introductory.

Johnson, David W. and Johnson, Frank P., *Joining Together: group theory and group skills* Prentice-Hall (paperback), 1975. pp. 470.
Exercises arranged in sections – leadership, groups, etc., and includes short theory sections.

Jongeward, Dorothy and James, Muriel, *Winning with People: group exercises in T.A.* Addison-Wesley (paperback), 1973. pp. 118.
Brief sections on theory with many individual and group exercises.

Pfeiffer, J. William and Jones, John E., *Annual Handbook for Group Facilitators 1972–1982* University Associates (ring-binder or paperback), 1972–82. 11 vols.
Each annual contains structured experiences, lecturettes, learning instruments, resources, theory and practise papers.

Pfeiffer, J. William and Jones, John E., *A Handbook of Structured Experiences* vols. I-VIII University Associates (ring-binder or paperback), 1974–81. 8 volumes.
Eight volumes contain 194 different training activities. Publishers actually encourage trainers to reproduce the material for training and educational purposes.

Maintaining Trainer Effectiveness

Cherniss, Cary, *Staff Burnout: job stress in the human services* Sage Publications, California (paperback), 1980. pp. 197.
Description of burnout – identifies both the individual traits and the

organisational factors which lead to burnout. Has a chapter on prevention.

Madders, Jane, *Stress and Relaxation* Third Edition Martin Dunitz (paperback), 1981. pp. 126.
Techniques of natural relaxation intended to reduce stress in everyday life. Exercises can obviously be introduced into appropriate training programmes.

Pines, Ayala M., Aronson, Elliot, Kafry, Ditsa, *Burnout: from tedium to personal growth* The Free Press, New York, 1981. pp. 229.
Description of burnout and coping strategies to combat the process in professional, family and interpersonal life.

Roon, Karin, *The New Way to Relax* World's Work Limited, 1951. pp. 257.
Practical handbook which offers techniques for releasing tension and using energy productively.

GLOSSARY OF TERMS

Bioenergetics
An approach to therapy developed by Alexander Lowen. The central belief of Bioenergetics is that the body can hold on to feelings and that they then affect muscle tension, posture and breathing patterns.

Burnout
Emotional and/or physical exhaustion leading to an inability to cope with the events of everyday life.

Co-counselling
An approach to counselling developed by Harvey Jackins which involves two people meeting at regular intervals to offer and receive counselling from each other. Now associated in the UK with John Heron.

Content
In the context of face-to-face communication, the words used and their literal meaning.

Encounter groups
Often used as a generic term; more specifically describes the approach associated with Will Schutz and involves using structured exercises as a way of identifying personal and interpersonal issues in a group.

Explicit process intervention
A considered and overt attempt by the trainer to help an individual

increase his awareness of himself and the quality of his relationships, particularly those within a training group.

Gestalt
The word 'Gestalt' is German and is difficult to translate precisely. An approximate translation is 'whole picture' or 'complete image'. See Appendix B for a description of the approach which was developed by Fritz Perls.

Good-Daddy, Bad-Daddy
A common process which occurs in training groups led by two or more tutors where one trainer is perceived as being good, kind, caring etc. while the other is perceived as tough, uncaring, brutal etc. It is often a manifestation of projection (see below).

'Here and now'
The feelings, behaviours, attitudes that are being expressed from moment to moment. Many feeling-based programmes use 'here and now' as the starting point for learning.

Hot-housing
Term used to describe what happens when members of a training group put pressure on themselves and others to have cathartic learning experiences.

Implicit process interventions
A considered attempt by the trainer covertly to affect

- the quality and nature of relationships within the group
- the feelings, attitudes and behaviour of individuals
- the relationship between himself and the group or an individual within it

Interpersonal Skills Training (IST)
A planned event intended to help somebody increase his awareness of himself and his impact on others.

Modelling
Involves the trainer using the skills, behaviours and attitudes that he is encouraging course members to use. Modelling is an implicit process intervention.

Personal process work
A joint activity between a trainer and a trainee in which the latter is helped to develop awareness of himself and the ways in which he

makes relationships, with particular attention paid to underlying meanings and feelings. Involves the trainer making a number of explicit process interventions.

Process
The feelings, values and motivation of the individual and the ways in which they are manifested, i.e.

- non-verbal behaviour
- regular patterns of verbal behaviour (e.g. argumentative, passive, despairing etc.)

Process intervention
An attempt by the trainer to affect directly

- the quality and nature of the relationships within the group
- the feelings, behaviours, attitudes of individuals
- the relationship between himself and the group

This attempt may be implicit or explicit.

Projection
Seeing in others qualities, attitudes and behaviours which the individual finds difficult to accept in himself.

Psychodrama
Approach developed by Jacob Moreno which involves using a detailed and elaborate role-play technique for developing awareness of self.

Sensitivity training
Generic term which encompasses a large number of training approaches e.g. T-group, Encounter Groups etc., and any number of hybrids.

Structural integration (Rolfing)
Approach developed by Ida Rolf which involves penetrating massage. A Rolfing programme consists of ten 1½ hours sessions.

T-group
The 'T' means training. Approach developed by Kurt Lewin which involves using an unstructured programme to learn, through experience, the processes which occur in groups.

'There and then'
Experiences, behaviours, feelings, attitudes that have occurred in

the past. Many interpersonal skills training programmes – particularly in the thinking/doing area – use the 'there and then' as the starting point for learning.

Transactional Analysis (TA)

Approach developed by Eric Berne which can be used across the thinking-doing-feeling spectrum. A transaction is a unit of communication comprising a statement and a response. For further details see Appendix A.

Unfinished business

The unresolved conflicts, unexpressed feelings, unsatisfied needs, that each individual brings to any relationship. The unfinished business may be from the recent or distant past or both.

Unstructured training

Term used to describe a number of feeling-based programmes which do not have a detailed programme e.g. IRO (see Table 4.1 p.59). In most cases there is a structure which course members have to discover.

INDEX